ODDS AGAINST EVENS

ODDS AGAINST EVENS
Young People and the Church

by ERNEST MARVIN

With an Introduction by
BRUCE KENRICK

The Westminster Press
Philadelphia

LIBRARY OF CONGRESS CATALOG CARD NO. 68–10459

PUBLISHED BY THE WESTMINSTER PRESS®

PHILADELPHIA, PENNSYLVANIA

PRINTED IN THE UNITED STATES OF AMERICA

Introduction

By Bruce Kenrick

WHEN ERNEST MARVIN bellowed, "Shut up!" from the pulpit of his Lockleaze church and the young man in the front pew stopped beating his girl's head with a hymnbook, I realized two things: First: he had succeeded in contacting the kind of youth who knew so little about the institutional Church that he felt free to bash his girl friend on the head at evening prayer. Second: his ministry of "acceptance" was no sugar-coated, irresponsible, live-and-let-live irrelevance; it was a ministry that respected people and took them so seriously that it was prepared to judge as well as to accept.

This, it seems to me, is fundamental to the dramatic advance of his work at Lockleaze. It was fundamental, also, to the work of Christ, who did not only say to the woman who had been taken in adultery, "I do not condemn you," but who also said, "Go, and sin no more."

And when on the Isle of Iona the tape of his play *A Man Dies* came to an end, I learned something from the moments that followed in which a small group of Iona Community men did not pitch in with our customary comments but were silent so that all one could hear through the open Abbey window was the faint sound of the waves down on the shore.

We were stunned. Stunned not only by the words and vibrant rhythm of the songs, by the devastating, inescapable interrelation between politics and faith, by the vivid revelation of the fact that Christ is crucified right here, right now by us in Rhodesia, Vietnam and Britain's slums—but above all by the profoundly moving fact that this revelation had come to us and many thousands more through young men and women from Ernest Marvin's church who were not by any means all convinced Christians but who, after acting out this painfully relevant passion play, could surely never be the same again.

Why do they come to church—these lighthearted, infuriating, wistfully seeking youngsters? Why come to this church and to so few besides?

In the first place, I'd say it is because this ministry began with very few preconceived ideas. Its principal preconception was that God was around not only in his Church but also in his world and that, maybe, if the Church would listen to what God would say through his world, that Church might learn how to become the Church in terms which that world would understand.

In the second place, I believe those youngsters come because those who minister to them have now won the right to be heard. They are not newcomers to the district who have no understanding of its problems; they don't focus on a pulpit-based ministry. They have made their home for more than ten years in the district; they are deeply involved in its total needs; they have worked hard for years to make Lockleaze a better place in which to live—they've won the right to be heard.

Third: they've made the Gospel visible. Not only audible but visible. They've done it in dramatic plays; they've done it in social action; they've done it in hours of discussion in pubs with leaders of local gangs. They preach the Gospel from the pulpit, to be sure. But they practice it in the streets as well. And sometimes men who are right outside the Church begin to respond when the Gospel is not only heard but seen.

As I write these words in the train, I have beside me the morning paper in which I read:

CHURCH ASSEMBLY ROUSED BY BOLD PETITION

A sense of urgency has been brought to the somewhat sedate proceedings of the General Assembly of the Presbyterian Church of England by a bold request to strengthen and expand the work in the Lockleaze area of Bristol. Contact on every conceivable front has been established; the work has flourished into a national testing ground. But the staff of two is grossly overworked and the only privacy the Reverend Ernest Marvin, the minister in charge, ever has is his bedroom. And even there he found someone sleeping in his bed one night. Lockleaze needs a team ministry of four and a grant of £20,000 to pay for accommodation.

And the exciting fact for me is this: A few years ago such a request would have stood the slenderest chance of success. Today, I'll be very surprised if the Presbyterian Church of England, despite its debts, its rising overheads and the in-numerable urgent calls on its funds—I'll be astonished if it doesn't produce a miracle involving four men and £20,000 ($56,000). And this fact is of infinitely wider significance than the parish of Lockleaze. It's a fact that reflects a rising tide of conviction in the church.

This conviction is that Christ was literally right when he cried, "Throw your life away, for it's the one way you'll gain it." More and more Christians believe that if their first con-cern is to protect the church plant, keep the funds out of the red and the pews well stocked, then they not only deserve to be lost but they are already lost. In increasing numbers they also believe that the Church is the one human grouping in the world that does not exist for the sake of its members but for the sake of those outside; that the Church's reason for being around is only to give its life away; and that only by thus ex-posing itself, by serving the world, by dying for the world, will the Church find that intoxicating life that God intends it to enjoy.

I believe the Church is moving into a new, exciting spring-time. This honest, gay, exhilarating book is a herald of spring for the Church everywhere—so long as it's wide awake.

Notting Hill,
London

Contents

Preface

THE MAIN concern of this book is with Teenagers and the Church. This is by no means an original topic and there are in existence today several works which amount almost to manuals containing worthwhile guidance for those in the Church who are making tremendous efforts to communicate with the young people of today.

This book is not an attempt to add to the number of such manuals, but is an account of what has happened over the last ten years at St James', in the post-war housing estate of Lockleaze, Bristol, England. Therefore what follows is mainly by way of description, with the occasional attempt at interpretation, and in no way do I wish to give the impression that we know all the answers to the many problems which face the Church and others in their attempts to engage in effective youth work.

In fact, here at St James' more young people have gone from than have remained within our walls, and when, from time to time, we have tried to appraise what we are doing, we do see that the 'expert' and professionally trained person might well be loath to dignify it with the term 'youth work.' In some years we have had as many as five hundred youngsters meeting on the premises in the course of a week, but then, almost imperceptibly, a new season begins and we wonder where they have all gone.

So the following pages are certainly not full of helpful hints on how to build up a youth club within the context of the Church and provide for it a programme which will ensure its everlasting success. They are simply an account of what has happened when a group of people of varying degrees of experience have tried to provide a meeting place for young people of numerous interests and backgrounds, and to give them a contact with the Church which otherwise they would not have had.

The title *Odds Against Evens* arises because this is a story neither of success nor of failure, but one which I hope might show how wide is the gap between young people and the Church today and also how important their presence is for the Church. I would like to think that what follows would illustrate that we are under no illusion about the size of the gap; and the title is meant to infer that the odds are always extremely high against the Church's ever breaking even or coming to terms with young people where they are. But despite this I am hopeful enough to believe that the effort has nonetheless been worthwhile. At the very least, the young people who have come and gone over the years have provided a necessary catalyst for the congregation. Certainly with their being present in the numbers they have been we have not been able to ignore the world, and they are a continual reminder of our mission to the world. Just as a catalyst helps forward a chemical reaction without itself suffering any chemical change, so the teenagers of St James' have helped to further and deepen our conception of the missionary and pastoral function of the Church, even though they themselves may not have been changed overmuch in the process.

Another reason for hesitating to write about the Church and young people is that it may give the impression that they are our only concern. This is far from being the case, but the terms of reference were to write on this specific topic. That other aspects of the work have not been given particular treatment does not mean that they are less important and are not taking place.

This book, of course, could not have been written if I had been left to my own devices. What it attempts to describe is the outcome of a shared experience with the people of St James', not least with my colleague, the Rev. Brian Phillips.

I would also like to acknowledge the help and advice of the Rev. Horace Allen, Warden of Iona Abbey, the Rev. Peter McCall, Trinity Presbyterian Church, Bristol, and the Rev. Neville Boundy, St Mary Redcliffe, Bristol.

Above all, I wish to place on record my appreciation for

the help received from Mr Mark Hankey, Headmaster of Clifton College Preparatory School. He has read the manuscript in its entirety and made many useful suggestions for which I am most grateful. But his participation has not simply been at an advisory level, and various chapters have had his hand upon them. I am particularly grateful to him for his research into the passion play letters and his collation of the same. Perhaps his Postcript is over-generous, but that is not for me to say.

Finally I would like to express appreciation of the indefatigable efforts of my secretary, Venetia Hunter. She has given much time and thought to the typing of the manuscript and indeed has helped greatly in planning its format and content.

1

Strategy for the Gap

I HAVE not been in many fights since I was ordained, but one or two stand out in the memory. There was, for instance, the night on which I hit George.

George had walked into the weekly dance without paying. George always tried to walk into the weekly dance without paying, but this time he was determined to get away with it. The man on door duty, an elder in the church, asked him for his half-crown. George's answer was to send him sprawling over a couple of chairs. Two seconds later my fist had landed squarely on George's jaw.

I do not know who was more surprised, George or I. At any rate the element of surprise was so great that it bereft George of any ability to retaliate. He simply leant against the wall, gasping and spluttering, transfixed with astonishment. I noticed, not without a certain pride, that his legs were decidedly wobbly.

When he had recovered some of his wind, he lurched forward a couple of steps and yelled in astonished indignation, "A f...ing Vicar 'it me! A f...ing Vicar 'it me! I don't believe in your f...ing God!" "So you don't believe in God?" I said. "Then why are you wearing that crucifix round your neck?" "Wearing what?" he said. "That crucifix," I said, pointing to the cheap piece of jewellery. He fingered it dubiously for a minute, then said "What's that got to do with God?"

Admittedly George is an extreme example of the problem that faces the Church in attempting to communicate with people today. But if we think his is a tall story, we are simply deluding ourselves.

Of course, for every George there are thousands of Toms. Dicks and Harrys who know that the Cross, Jesus and God are all related to each other because the Bible and the Church say so. But equally they do not consider them to be of any present significance. What do they think of Christ? He was a very good man, perhaps the best. Maybe he was the Son of God. But so what?

Admittedly I have begun with an example which is extreme, though by no means unique. It is necessary to do so because so many Christians seem to think that the 'so what?' can be answered by bigger and better techniques. If only, it is thought, we could stumble upon the right method of communication, that would be at least a beginning.

But the right method of communicating what? We cannot avoid methods and techniques, and it is right and proper that we should search for good ones. The right method, however, has to be used for the right purpose and it is precisely at this point that confusion arises. Good and valid methods of communicating religion are not necessarily good and valid for communicating a faith, a way of life. Christianity is not a religion, although religion is an important part of it. This distinction must be kept firmly in mind, for it has led to a great confusion about the use of techniques.

The cart is constantly put before the horse. In recent times much commendable time and effort has been spent by a variety of Christians in the search for relevant modern methods. But often enough this search has in the main been concentrated on trying to communicate religion, as opposed to the wider issue of trying to communicate the faith. So it is that never before in the Church's history have there been such tremendous efforts to popularize religion. Much time is spent on refurbishing our liturgies, our literature, our doorstep evangelism, our notice-boards, our hymns and all the rest. But no matter how ably the Gospel is expressed in twentieth-century language and how cleverly we work out a people's liturgy which even a child can understand, it is significant that the people to whom such efforts mainly appeal are those who are already within the

Church. Techniques which are solely concerned with the religious side of the faith have been extremely helpful where some church members are concerned, and in particular for youngsters who, through no fault of their own, have found themselves in church families and who are in danger of being 'dragged up' in the faith until of an age to rebel once and for all.

It is right and proper we should continue to pay attention to religious techniques. But we must recognize that George and his counterparts are simply not within range of this type of method, valid though it is within certain prescribed limits. You cannot use religious techniques to communicate the faith anew to those who have never had it, whether young or old.

The much more fundamental problem is how to demonstrate that Christianity is an all-embracing way of life and is not concerned only with that part of it which goes on in church. The horse must be put squarely in front of the cart. How then can this be done?

The old cliché states that a faith can only be caught, not taught. Like all good clichés it is an over-simplification, but it is a useful point from which to begin. Strategy now comes into its own in the attempt to create the conditions within which a faith can be caught. The faith must begin with people and progress through people. 'The church did not create individuals; it was the individuals who created the church. Yet the individuals could not have accomplished their work without the church. Joined in these two circular sentences is the real truth. Churches live by individuals; individuals are, or should be, served by churches.'[1] An initial consideration therefore, must be to take into account the places where people meet, in or out of church, for it is people who matter above everything else. There have to be meeting grounds where the faith can be caught, but we must not make the mistake of thinking that these places must be confined to church premises. If we are simply aiming to transport people from one area of relation-

[1] A. Q. Morton and James McLeman, *Christianity and the Computer*, Hodder and Stoughton, 1964, p. 78.

ship to another, we can fail to make use of the opportunities afforded by those which they are already enjoying.

A great deal depends upon the local area and the pattern that has emerged there, with or without benefit of clergy. There are many parishes within which the church is the only, not just the best, example of a community within which personal relationships of any depth have a chance to flourish. There are, however, many more where the local church would certainly not be the first grouping to come to mind when one looks for a real expression of life in a community. The situation in which the Christian finds himself should decide the strategy he will choose in order to communicate his faith. This is a much more relevant procedure than that of evolving a technique to transfer people from their area to his area, with no thought as to whether they wish to be so transferred.

Incidentally, it is sad to note the cries of delight which have arisen when two or more congregations have united in one larger congregation. This is often looked upon as an advance of the faith and hailed as an act of witness. 'Witness to what?' one wonders. Two thousand years' crass stupidity and lack of love? That may well be. But it is no more a witness to the outsider that the church is now possessed of a stronger faith than the decision of two old age pensioners to live together is a guarantee of renewed vigour. The champions of one such united church, where three congregations combined, proudly stated that one group had to sacrifice its building, another its hymn book and the third its hall. If this is what we count as sacrifice, no wonder the world does not take us seriously and does not consider that we provide a place where worthwhile relationships can occur. If you join one senile body to another, the result is not strength but greater weakness. This may seem a little harsh. I may react emotionally to the ballyhoo which accompanies such events and which can blind us to the fact that, although our religious techniques may now be in better trim, the state of the faith in relation to the world is no further advanced.

We should not, initially at any rate, be over-anxious about

getting people into church or about combining churches. Our major task must be with the faith and not religion, and our strategy should be mainly concerned with discovering where the meeting grounds actually are. We should start from there. This is not to decry the importance of religion or of what goes on in church. It is important. But 'what we do in church is only the social part of our religion and must ever be the secondary part. It is the part which is easiest to discuss and codify and so will always be the part most favoured by writers and teachers, but only rarely is it the first part for anyone.[2]

There are, I believe, two main ways open to the Church in her attempt to be Christ to the world. By Church, I am thinking here of the small nucleus of committed Christians found in most places and not just of the parson. This group forms a cell and the choice of method which they must adopt in the light of their local situation depends on their area of operations, the body within which they are the cell and the lump wherein they have to work as leaven.

In *The New Reformation?*[3] the Bishop of Woolwich describes one of the Christian's tasks today as that of being 'the gracious neighbour'. But what is the area within which we are to practise loving, neighbourly concern? The Bishop emphasizes that this concern must be expressed outside the building. This cannot be over-stressed, when too many Christians still consider that all that really matters happens within the confines of the sanctuary. But the problems that arise through expressing Christian neighbourliness are no less a challenge for having to be hammered out on church premises. If, as in our own case in Bristol, a wide cross-section of a housing area of sixteen thousand people finds most of its weekday life revolving in and around the church building, then we need look no further for the area within which we are to be the leaven. The opportunities for full-time discipleship are to be found not only on our doorstep but within the house itself. I

[2] Ibid., p. 81.
[3] John A. T. Robinson, Bishop of Woolwich, *The New Reformation?*, SCM Press Ltd, 1965.

shall talk about this in the next chapter. It is one of the ways open to the Church of today to fulfil her vocation to people. We must not despise a crowded church and one with an active, organized life. The cell needs a crowd within which to operate.

The second way in which the Church can act as a cell is one which should be within the scope of all of us, whether we have a large congregation or not. It is to seek out the groupings within which some kind of personal encounter is already taking place. In most parishes there are in existence organizations and liaisons which some churches, to their shame, ignore. These bodies can be anything from a local youth club to a community centre. A number of housing estates are possessed of community centres which are supported by public funds and often have a full-time, salaried staff. Their activities range from nursery playgrounds and youth clubs to cultural pursuits and adult social clubs. They are open every day of every week. It would be impossible and wrong for the church to compete with the more successful of these. But here is a ready-made opportunity for the cell to function. Here people are meeting each other and are already experiencing relationships at varying levels.

A ministerial colleague works in a parish similar to my own, where he has a worshipping congregation of about twenty people out of a possible fifteen thousand. But he himself is secretary of the local community association and runs their youth club. His two churchwardens are managers of that association, and several of the faithful twenty are active organizers in it. He knows that this involvement will not necessarily bring more people into his church, but he is not trying to bring people into church; indeed he is embarrassed when some people, in response to his friendship and concern for them, threaten to repay it by coming along to the evening service. The day may come when such a threat will be better received, but the church is not yet ready for it.

It is people who matter first and foremost, and in many situations such as his, where secular bodies are already well established, the Church must rejoice that such opportunities

16

exist. Having gathered its members for worship once a week as a cell, it should thereafter be the Body where people are. This is the only point from which the Church can begin in many of our housing areas. It is perhaps a less glamorous way than the one we are used to in Lockleaze. It is nice to have a full church with all the concomitant external trappings. Yet neither approach is necessarily more effective than the other. Often indeed the trappings and the external signs of a successful congregation disguise the true enormity of the task and give rise to premature congratulations.

At the time of writing, those of us who constitute the cell at St James', Lockleaze, are very conscious that these trappings can be shaky. Even on those occasions when we have gone months at a time with a packed church and an apparently flourishing community life, we have painfully learnt not to make too many sweeping claims about the advance of the Gospel and the making of Christians. Both methods, the cell involving itself in the community outside the buildings and the cell involving itself in the community which has come within range of the buildings, pose very similar problems.

What I am now attempting to describe is really a case of wisdom after the event. We did not start by looking at the parish situation as it was and then deciding which kind of cell we would be. We began by assuming that we should attempt to get people into church. That we succeeded to a limited extent is a fact, but that we should have attempted to do so is open to question. However, this is how we began. We cannot begin again. But looking back, I can see that we were not seeking a congregation within which we could be the leaven. Rather we were anxious for a large lump of pew-fodder.

The group which initially came into the church as a result of our efforts was not on the whole an adult one. Adults tend to be set in their ways and, even for a football match or a social occasion, can only with difficulty be prised away from their cars, firesides or television sets. The church is certainly no better as an alternative enticement. The only ones not static in their ways were and are the teenagers. They became the target, although they were by no means sitting ducks. Their arrival on the grand scale is described in the chapter which follows. But let it be said now that it was they who quite early on, as the unexpected and unsuspecting catalyst, forced us into the role which we now play, that of a cell within the church building.

But now that this has happened, and with the wisdom which hindsight always affords, we would suggest that such a pattern could be repeated elsewhere, and at this point strategy and know-how are vital. Chapter Two may be of assistance in describing the lines this strategy should take. One cannot dispense with technique, even when the initial ball has been set rolling. Whether it be called 'playing it by ear' or what you will, once begun the situation requires constant application.

And it *is* skilled work, despite what Graham said when he stood in the middle of the church hall one night with his open wage packet in his hand. He was just nineteen and worked for British Railways. It was Friday night, pay night. He was proud of what he had earned, especially as there had been plenty of overtime. A group of admiring teenagers had gathered round at his bidding to see the figure for themselves. From the edge of the group I caught a glimpse of the pay slip. which registered £17 10s. 3d. "That, Graham," I said rather querulously, "is more than I earned last week." There was a pause as he looked at me in some surprise. "Well, yes," he answered, "but this is skilled work."

As an additional commentary on the image of the church as held by many a youngster, it was a revealing remark. But the irony of such statements is that Graham and his friends would not be around to make them if it had not been for much skilful labour on the part of a group of committed people who happened to call themselves Christians.

2

Oil and Water

"OF COURSE, all they do at Lockleaze is rock 'n roll."
We have heard this stated so often now that it no longer
irritates. Anyway, those who talk today about 'rock 'n roll'
simply show how out of date they are. But two factors have
helped to give the impression that our brides twist down
the aisle to hotted-up versions of the Wedding March and
that our congregations prefer Beat to Bach. One is the nature
of our youth work, which includes a Sunday night club, and
the other is our passion play set to modern music, called *A
Man Dies*.[1] The play will be mentioned later. In this chapter
I wish to describe our attempt to bring young people into the
worship of the church via the Sunday night club.

We began, as I have explained, by believing that it was
good to attempt to bring them into the church and that they
would be easier to influence than their parents. Another
reason for making them the target was that young people as a
group are, on the whole, more noticeable by their absence
from the church. The church is supposed to be a family. It
can better claim to be such if members are present at all levels
and ages.

Many a parson who has been exposed to what Provost Ernest
Southcott calls 'pew-monia' knows the debilitating effects of a
small congregation, no matter how faithful the few may be. It
can be shattering, especially if he is a comparative novice
straight from college and raring to show them a thing or two.
Small wonder if some clerics are glad to hit upon a gimmick

[1] Published by Darton, Longman and Todd, 1964.

which might do the trick. 'Pop Services' are examples of such a gimmick, but so also are 'Your Favourite Hymn' Services, 'Question and Answer' Services, not to mention Harvest Festival Services. Such gimmicks have no permanent effect on attendances; there has been plenty of proof of that in these last years.

If at St James' we had relied on the gimmick of pop music, we would have failed long ago to make any kind of relevant impact upon the community around about us and should probably have lost what congregation we had. This congregation, after a very long period without a Minister, was not strong numerically, though it contained a small group of people who today are still amongst the most faithful members. Only a handful of young people attended occasionally, but there was an open youth club, which met on Thursday evenings, and enjoyed a fair measure of success. In the new housing areas, before the arrival downtown of the commercial boys, such as Top Rank, and of everything from ice rinks to discothèques, almost anybody could have opened a hall in the middle of a housing estate – 'worse than a graveyard with lights'[2] – set up a table-tennis table and a record-player, and have been assured of some kind of success, even if one hesitated to dignify such activities as 'youth work'. It was after one such Thursday night club that I made the announcement "This club will now meet on Sunday night as well. First, we shall meet at 6.30 p.m. at evening service, along with the rest of the church family, and then in the hall afterwards, when the usual club activities will take place. But" – and here came the crunch – "if you want to come to the second half, you are expected to come to the first." Up went the cry "Bribery!" We admit it could be construed as such, but our experience over the years has convinced us that it is by no means corruption! The youngsters don't have to come at all if they do not wish to do so.

At that time I had been Minister of St James' for almost a year. There had been time enough for me to be convinced in my own mind that even if I were to remain in the parish for

[2] Youngster reporting to the Albemarle Committee.

twenty years, and be accepted along with the other few members by successive generations of young people as a reasonable sort of person, despite my back-to-front collar, if I were able to go into the homes, the pubs and the community centres and be greeted as a friend, if I were able to win their confidence and be accepted almost as one of themselves, if I were able to do all that and more and *then* ask them to come to church, they would still have refused. No ice would have been broken, only a polite but distant contact would have been made. Their attitude would have been 'The Vicar only wants us to go to his building. We don't want to go, so we must keep him at arm's length.'

The barriers of many years were up and the great temptation in the face of such barriers was certainly to remain inside other people's constricting view of what the Church should be and to retreat into a congregation that was wholly inward-looking and which could have no effect on the rest of the parish. If there had been a ballet society on the estate, they could not have been expected to be in a narrower confine. Such lack of contact may mean that the Church can exist quite happily in its own cocoon, but this must mean that, instead of being the salt which leavens the lump, it becomes the salt which is in the blue twisted paper of the old-fashioned packet of potato crisps.

Many teenagers feel, however wrongly, that the Church only wants them in to be preached at, to occupy the same bit of polished wood each week, to be units added to the weekly freewill offering scheme, and not to make a contribution in their own way. They are not therefore likely to darken so much as the grass outside the church door, unless drastic action is taken.

The problem, as it appeared to us, was how to get the oil and the water into the same barrel. It seemed insuperable. So it was that we attempted to conjoin a Sunday club with the evening service and make attendance at the former dependent on attendance in church. It must be said that it has never been a rigid rule. And the difference between a guiding principle and a concrete and hard-and-fast rule has not always been

21

grasped by some of the older ones who sometimes urge a rigid enforcement of a law which has never existed in fact.

On the very first Sunday of the new club results could be seen. Groups of youngsters came to the service and quite rapidly in the weeks that followed the whole thing snowballed, sometimes in an alarming way. In the first few years of this 'experiment' the church was jammed with young people, with an occasional overflow into the large hall next door. These were the days when there were no alternative attractions except that of watching the telly with Mum, Dad, the cat and the canary. It could be said we had it easy, though that is not the way members of the congregation would describe it who, time after time, found worship to be a shattering rather than an uplifting experience.

Nowadays the rule is still basic to a Sunday night, but with the passing of the teenage bulge, the advancing age of the estate and the plethora of pursuits open to young people every night of the week, things are not quite so 'easy' as once they were. Often enough, in the winter time especially, the church is full and two-thirds of the congregation is made up of young people. In other weeks they do not come. Today teenage attendance on a Sunday has to be worked for to a degree that was unnecessary before. But the Sunday night 'rule' is still a useful basis.

It was significant that the young people began to come to church in groups and not as individuals. This gave them the necessary courage to step through the strange doors of a church building, amongst the unfamiliar hats and hymn books. The 'rule' enabled them to save face in front of their friends, who would otherwise have poured withering scorn upon the mere suggestion of going to church. It is interesting to observe how even today face is saved in this way by many a youngster who does not want to admit to attending church of his own free will.

There are many stories that could be told to illustrate that, though in one sense we were able to collect a congregation, in another they brought a host of problems with them. By all accepted standards their conduct in church has on occasions been deplorable. In the early days, when the estate was still being built, roads were incomplete and all was mud and chaos, there was a great deal of mobility to and from the area by families who could not or would not settle. The general unrest of the time resulted for a few years in some children being wilder than they have ever been since. This found expression in the church service. On at least two occasions I can remember hymn books being flung around during worship. That the congregation held together and put up with similar goings-on is to their credit, though we have at times been driven pretty close to the point of a breakdown in personal relationships.

Only one member has left the church because of the behaviour of young people. It happened one hot summer evening. Bernice walked down the aisle and sat down with a bump in a pew. She kicked off her stiletto heels, hitched her skirt over her knees and placed her aching feet on the pew in front. She turned to the middle-aged man sitting next to her and said, "Cor, ain't it bloody 'ot?" He left immediately and he has not been back since. In fact it *was* bloody hot, and Bernice was just trying to be friendly in the only way she knew. Moreover, her greeting was in sharp distinction from the lack of welcome she received from him in the House of the Lord. Other adults have been driven close to despair at times by the unexpected, 'out of place' happenings, but it is to their credit that they still remain to tell the tale.

In the Preface I wrote that the young provide a catalyst. The story of Bernice illustrates this. They force us to examine our faith and to test its validity in concrete situations. We began to learn that it is no use to talk about the great truths of the gospel, such as God's forgiveness and his acceptance of the likes of us, sinners though we are, if we are not prepared to show even a fraction of that same kind of acceptance towards the Bernices of the world.

Then of course there was Dennis, who walked down the aisle before the evening service began with his transistor radio set blaring out the latest hit tune. When an elder remonstrated with him, the honest, bewildered, slightly defensive answer was "The Service ain't begun yet." This of course was true, but even with generations of Free Church pre-service chatter, which usually only ceases when the Minister appears in the pulpit, behind us, such conduct still came as something of a shock. But there again one has to say to the puzzled elder, "If Christ died for us while we were yet sinners, one of the implications is that we have at the very least to accept the Dennises of this world with their transistor radios blaring away in and out of church." In fact, the logic of the gospel is unanswerable.

Another final illustration of the many which demonstrate how we have had to steel ourselves against the unexpected, concerns the arrival of the two small girls and the Alsatian dog. This took place during the singing of the hymn before the sermon. The deacons at the door argued with them, stating that the dog could not be brought in to the service. This caused such anguish of heart to the young girls, who said that they could not walk all the way home with the dog, that the deacons, in desperation, suggested that the animal should be tied up outside and then they would be allowed to enter. They agreed to this, and within moments had returned. Now, after the sermon the offering is taken, and when it got to the two ladies in question, another dispute broke out, in which the very same deacons were involved. "You don't expect us," they shrilled, "to give to that as well?" "As well as what?" replied a flustered office-bearer, trying to keep the volume of the conversation down. "As well as lock our dog in the public lavatory across the road," replied the elder of the two.

I would not like to give you the impression this kind of happening is a weekly occurrence. With the more settled nature of the parish the youngsters themselves are better behaved. But we still have our moments, and occasionally one or other of the Ministers has to interrupt a lesson, a prayer or a sermon to tell certain recalcitrants in no uncertain terms to shut up.

The fact that the teenagers have come in such large numbers cannot, of course, be a justification in itself of this bribery without corruption. But we continually point out to critics of this scheme that the choice to come or not to come still rests with the youngster. He need not come at all if he does not wish to do so. The idea that it is right because it works carries no weight, because the initial reason why the teenagers come is not to worship. But a first contact is made, and if the youngsters feel at the start that the price of a short service is not too high a payment for an evening mainly spent in the way they like, then both sides are satisfied. It does not work in the sense that the teenager soon comes to learn what it is to worship the Lord joyfully (there are a large number of adults who plough on worshipping in the hope that an odd glimpse will be given to them of what real and alive worship can be). But they do learn fairly soon that within and behind the Church are a small number of people who care for them, who are more than ready to listen to them and to offer an unshockable ear whenever and wherever it is asked for and needed. The main justification for this 'bribery' seems to me to be this: that the Church can and does get itself into the position of showing in practice that it cares.

Things would be far worse than they are if the evening service did not appeal at any point whatsoever to the young-sters who come. If there is nothing in it that holds them, if at no point are they made to feel they have a part to play, then no matter how good the club is afterwards, I am convinced they would not continue to come as they have. It would, of course, have been asking for trouble to have imposed upon them (or upon the adults, for that matter) too traditional a pattern of worship. The Prayer Book was out, and so was the Free Church 'hymn sandwich'. As it is, we are by no means satisfied with the form of worship that has developed over these last years; but at least we believe it has developed out of a living situation and it has to be judged accordingly.

They bring to the service their liveliness and their impatience and their anxiety to be entertained. It may start as, and, in the mind of the youngsters themselves, continue to be, entertain-ment as most of us think of it. Entertainment is something to be enjoyed, like 'Sunday Night at the London Palladium' or a thriller or a western. But the original sense of entertainment was something that enters into the mind and becomes part of the way of thinking or understanding, one facet of life. This may be only temporary. But it can be permanent. The evidence is that, probably unconsciously, the service does for many become entertainment in the rarer sense of the word. This of course is the same argument which is used to justify 'compulsory' worship elsewhere, and the truism that no one can know just what is sinking in is no less true of the housing-estate than it is of the public school chapel.

'Liturgy' means 'the work of the people'. For a service to have any chance of coming alive those present must actively participate in it. We have seen that they can be very lively and noisy in church, but the problem is how can they participate in the actual worship? Many of them, even at the age of eighteen, have never been in church before, except perhaps in their mothers' arms.

Some theologians would insist that it is necessary for at least some element of faith to be present in those who attend a church service to which corporate worship is the natural response. But although it is true that the presence of faith in Jesus Christ as Lord is an excellent starting-point for worship, it need not be the only starting-point.

An important part of liturgy is offering, the offering of ourselves just as we are. We offer ourselves to him, so that he can refashion us as his Body and send us out to be broken in service on the world. Now the self we habitually offer could be described as a Sunday self, often not quite the same as, often totally different from, our Monday to Saturday self. The offering we make on Sunday usually consists of the praise of our lips, the intentions of our hearts and of course the giving of a little of our money. It does not necessarily involve us in a bringing of ourselves as we really are to the altar. 'Just as I am without one plea' is by no means always a true statement of the facts.

When we enter the church it is so easy to leave our real selves behind, as easy as it is for the Moslem entering his mosque to leave his shoes behind. But a typical youngster of today is not able to make this distinction, and it is this fact which I believe has provided the starting-point for our evening worship at Lockleaze.

So, over the years, despite many shows of reluctance, the teenagers have come to church. The attendance has varied. During a 'good' winter season, lasting from the end of October until the middle of March, if we are lucky we can have over a hundred and fifty of them at the evening service. A poorer season will see no more than fifty present. But fifty is still a large enough number to enable them to retain their identity as a group and to act as the all-important catalyst. We have to take them as they are and it is from this point that our worship begins.

It has been unusual to see many coming just for the service and then going off for the rest of the evening. Many of the older ones shake hands with the Ministers at the door and then go across to the pub and come back for the last hour of the club. Those who are walking out and going steady do in fact walk out, which only goes to prove that the service has come to mean something and that, given the right company, even the plainest of streets can become a paradise garden!

3

Liturgy – the Work of the People

IT IS all very well to write in general terms, but I must now be more specific and describe what we actually do at these services. I propose in this chapter to give an outline of a typical evening service. I am sure that when it is read in cold print it will seem traditional and orthodox and so a preliminary word of explanation may be advisable.

Worship should not be left to the whim of the individual. It must be approached with theology and tradition, as well as the world we live in, very much in mind. But in many of our churches (and I think this is particularly true of the Free Churches) we have tended to be subjective and intellectual in our approach to it. Free Church worship is usually in the hands of the Minister to the final amen. And most services still seem to pivot around the sermon, which can last for anything from fifteen minutes to an hour.

I deeply believe in the importance of what Carnegie Simpson described as 'the monstrance of the Word'. By monstrance is normally meant a transparent vessel in which the consecrated Host is displayed for adoration or carried in procession. But by talking about the monstrance of the Word, Simpson was stressing the importance in worship of a clear showing forth and declaration of the mighty acts of God and of his love for us in Jesus Christ.

In much Free Church worship we tend in practice, if not in theory, to identify this monstrance solely with the preaching. The first part of the service still seems to be treated as a preliminary to the all-important sermon. Another confusion is to equate the Word with that which is spoken as distinct from that which is done, acted and demonstrated in visual form. But the liturgy must be seen to be an overall activity within which preaching is an important part but one not to be emphasized at the expense of the rest. Nor is it confined to the spoken word.

Admittedly the conventional Free Church building can be a great barrier to real congregational worship, a boxing ring for a pulpit, and everybody seeming to worship the organ pipes. But it need not be an insurmountable barrier. The most hideous buildings can be, and often are, places where a real encounter takes place between a man and his God.

In a modern housing estate, of course, such Victoriana are quite out of place. Architecture is important. Although St James', Lockleaze, is not an outstanding example of modern architecture, at least it is only fifteen years old, is compact and 'worshipful'. The Table is central, the pulpit, without being out on a limb, is to the side, and the font is obvious to the eye on the other side of the chancel.

In the chancel there is space to move around. Movement in front of and within such a congregation is essential, as much for psychological as for liturgical reasons. We do not actually use a trapeze. But movement there should be, so long as it is not fussy. Many a Free Church Minister knows the advantage of perambulating his pulpit. Why not his chancel?

Today many people find it hard to concentrate for long, whether they are reading a book or watching television. In our evening service this is borne very much in mind. Although the service incorporates an introit, two sets of prayers, three lessons, a creed, four hymns, notices, the sermon and an offering (as a separate part of the service), is it usually over in forty-five minutes. The accent is on brevity, speed and movement.

In much of our worship we tend to over-pray, praying too often and too long. Shorter prayers have more chance of being listened to and therefore prayed. Readings especially must be short and, where possible, taken from modern translations and

29

paraphrases. The whole service flows along – some would say races along, but why not? – with hardly a pause between one part and the next. Faced with the mixed congregation of Lock-leaze, amongst whom some are present under duress, any silence lasting longer than three seconds may be filled by impromptu contributions from members of the congregation. On one occasion, when I began the service with the scriptural injunction "Jesus said, I am the way, the truth and the life", I took longer than usual to announce the hymn which followed, and in the two seconds' grace that was given, a voice from the back pew was heard to say, "Well, he was a big-head then." It is the kind of comment that can shatter the mood. At the same time, like many such comments, it was not without relevance to what had been said.

Your committed churchman may know how to use silence. There is certainly room for it in worship. But there is not much room for it in this particular kind of evening service. On Sundays we have a communion service at 9 a.m. which is for the church members as such. Here of course there is more room for the meditative and contemplative approach. If we had only our evening 'thing', then the worship would be truncated and incomplete, but the day has to be seen as a whole. This accords pretty closely with early Church practice, when the faithful met in the morning for the breaking of bread and the later service was looked upon as the missionary one to which the catechumens and the fringe were invited.

This does not mean to say we have not had and cannot have our moments of silence at night. When there has been a real sense of need or a grief shared locally, when babies have been baptized, as they often are in the evening in front of the congregation, then there has been an atmosphere which defies description. These moments are few and far between, but that they happen at all is indication enough that worship is within the ability of anyone.

Speed, movement and brevity, conjoined to a 'reasonable' theology, are essential ingredients. This does not mean that there has to be a compromise with the orthodox shape of the liturgy. The pattern of our service is as in most orthodox Presbyterian churches, where there is a deep respect for order and natural progression in worship. It begins with praise and adoration, proceeds through confession, and so on to the closing benediction. Although the majority of the congregation are probably not aware that it has a shape, they would be the poorer for its absence. Even the most casual youngster, without being able to articulate this, can sense when there is order as opposed to bits and pieces. There need not be any conflict with the shape of the liturgy as evolved traditionally. It is in what happens within the pattern that we begin to see differences of approach from standard practice.

The language has to be pretty basic without catering for the lowest common denominator. In his book on preaching, the Bishop of Guildford[1] told a young parson who was to preach to a cathedral congregation, "Preach to the choirboys". If you are trying to make something relevant and comprehensive to the teenager, it is also relevant and comprehensible to the adults. Like everything else, worship has to be shared and for the Christian should not be a time for escape into a dream world of unusual phrases. 'Thees' and 'thous' are out, even in a West Country setting. A common criticism of addressing God as 'you' is that it is being all-matey with the Almighty. But it depends on how it is done and especially on the context within which it is done. If we are trying in our worship to express not only the transcendence of God but also his immanence, then the use of everyday speech can be helpful. One could tentatively say that the actual language used communicates his immanence and the way in which it is phrased his transcendence.

At the beginning of the evening service the first aim is to arrest the attention of the gathered throng, many of whom, minutes before, have stubbed out their cigarettes in the church porch, clattered down the steps into the pews, greeted their friends, changed places several times and are still engaged in conversation when the Ministers arrive at the main entrance.

[1] George Reindorp, *Putting it Over*, Hodder and Stoughton, 1961.

At this point they need something to do and see. So, on the first note of the Doxology 'All praise to Thee, my God, this night', they get to their feet and sing it while a large Bible is carried in through the main entrance of the church by an elder, followed by the two Ministers. This 'procession' passes down the aisle and by the end of the final verse of the Doxology faces the congregation in line, the elder still holding the Bible. One Minister says 'The Lord be with you' and the congregation replies 'And with you'. We had ceased to use the response 'And with your spirit' before we noticed that 'And with you' was also common practice in modern Roman Catholic liturgies. It makes what we are about to do much more immediate and personal. After all when we meet each other in the street and say "How are you?" we do not expect the reply, "Fine, and how's your spirit?"

Immediately after the responsive greeting there is a scripture sentence, then a hymn of praise, with no amens unless they are called for musically. During this hymn the elder places the Bible on the Communion Table, on which there are already a chalice and the alms dish. As the last note is still on everybody's lips, they are commanded to pray. At this point a very few kneel, the majority take up a conventional Free Church shampoo crouch position, and others, mainly youngsters, sit bolt upright and stare boldly round them at the peculiar antics of their neighbours. This is one reason for encouraging members to kneel. It is an act of witness in front of a host of observers. I agree with the view that a man should pray in the position in which he is least conscious of his body, but at the same time he must also be conscious of the Body.

The first prayer consists of a short act of adoration. This is followed by a short prayer of confession, then the response 'Lord have mercy upon us, Christ have mercy upon us, Lord have mercy upon us.' Thereafter the other Minister pronounces the absolution according to the Taizé rite, 'May each one of you acknowledge himself to be indeed a sinner, humbling himself before God, and believe that it is the Father's will to have mercy upon him in Jesus Christ; to all who thus repent and seek Jesus Christ for their salvation, I declare the absolution of their sins in the name of the Father and of the Son and of the Holy Ghost. Amen.' As this is being said, the sign of the Cross is made – again something seen and witnessed by many who have not participated in the actual prayer. The congregation say the amen and almost before they are able to join the younger members in a sitting position the Old Testament lesson has begun. This is done with the minimum of introduction. There is as yet no tradition of following the readings in one's own Bible.

The Old Testament does provide many problems. We often make do by simply reading a psalm, or part of a psalm, especially in the Gélineau translation. After about ten verses one senses the ebbing away of whatever concentration there has been. But just as feet begin to shuffle and remarks become more audible, one Minister says amen and heads turn, à la Wimbledon, to the opposite side of the chancel where the other announces the Letter. The switch from one to the other helps to re-focus attention. Occasionally they not only put up with eight, nine or ten more verses but actually listen to them. When the Letter is concluded and the Gospel about to be read, a little more action has to be introduced, as they have already sat through a prayer and two lessons. This is provided by announcing 'Let us prepare to hear the Holy Gospel'. All stand and sing the verses by Patrick Appleford:

> Go into all the world,
> Jesus is sending us,
> His new commands he tells us to teach,
> His saving Cross and victory preach,
> That all men may be baptized in Jesus once sacrificed;
> Dying with him and rising again,
> Gladly we worship with the refrain,
> > Praise be to you O Christ,
> > Praise be to you, O Christ.[2]

[2] In *Thirty 20th Century Hymn Tunes*, Joseph Weinberger Ltd, 1960.

The tune is lively and modern but seems to suit all tastes. The Gospel, again usually no more than ten verses, is then read from the chancel steps while the congregation remain standing. This provides a useful opportunity to stretch the legs and to tune in once more.

As the amen to the Gospel is said, the command is given: 'Let us declare our faith in the Apostles' Creed.' Here we say the Creed with one or two emendations of a minor variety, such as replacing 'the quick' with 'the living'. This is not the place to go over the old arguments, beloved by Free Church folk, for and against credal statements, but I do feel that a corporate declaration of faith is useful, especially in our situation. Until there is something better, we shall continue to use the Apostles' Creed. But we do recognize that parts of this Creed cannot be accepted with integrity by some Christians, including myself, as they stand. So it is that the congregation declare 'We believe' as opposed to 'I believe'. This is a recognition that we are a family, united in principle but begging to differ on details. There are a few present who can accept the Creed as it is, but even they recognize that there are others who cannot. So it is in this mood that we say 'we', recognizing it as a corporate declaration, an attempt to express the beliefs of a variety of people who are at different stages in their Christian pilgrimage. It is also an indication of our dependence upon the faith of the Church through the ages.

Saying the Creed has provided yet another opportunity for an act of witness in front of our ever-present catalyst.

After the Creed we move straight into a hymn, during the last verse of which one Minister moves down the centre aisle to take the prayers of thanksgiving and intercession from the body of the church. As every Anglican knows, this symbolizes the fact that these are the prayers of the whole church and not just of a Minister. But it has the added advantage of refocusing attention yet again and occasionally quietening some talkative youngsters now within range of a righteous arm. These prayers are followed by the Lord's prayer, during which the Minister walks back to the chancel. If he did not get there before the prayer was finished, short though the aisle is, there would be a dangerous pause of a few seconds in which anything could happen. But when the congregation awake, he has rejoined his colleague in front of them.

At this point the notices dealing with all aspects of the life of the following week, including football matches and Bible studies, are given, together with the usual invitation to all present, not just the young people, to partake of refreshment at the end of the service. The hymn preceding the sermon is announced, during which the Minister goes to the pulpit. At the end of the hymn he invokes in no uncertain terms the Triune Name. It has to be done in no uncertain terms to try to impress that something worth while is about to happen, to cover up his own feelings of inadequacy at this point and also to take the place, initially at least, of a text.

I would certainly not like to give the impression by what follows that I consider myself to be an accomplished preacher. But perhaps after ten years of preaching in this particular situation one is qualified to make a few observations, if only to point out lessons learnt from one's mistakes.

Preaching must be reasonably brief. I know only a few men who can hold the attention of a congregation for a considerable time, in some instances for almost an hour. Such men are, however, helped by preaching to a large number of the converted who like that sort of thing. But when you are engaged in building up a congregation, such preaching seems out of place, to say the least. Of course there are exceptions to every rule. When Dr George MacLeod last preached on one of his rare visits he did so for twenty-two minutes. Although well able to use simple language, he chose on that occasion to express himself in philosophical and theological terminology. But the assembled throng sat enraptured. Perhaps only George MacLeod could get away with it. He has a great presence, enhanced by his scarlet Queen's Chaplaincy cassock, which underlines the importance of the visual in worship.

Most sermons are planned with the young people in mind. This is unavoidable, especially in the winter when they predominate, and I think it is also legitimate. There was an Anglican chaplain to a university who felt that sermons planned with university students in mind would be totally unacceptable to the normal parishioners. But they for their part were thankful that they were treated as intelligent human beings and were given a rest from the normal jargon and clichés. By preaching with the teenagers in mind, you are not running the risk of by-passing the normal listener, even by over-simplification. The young people themselves would be the first to see through this and know that you were talking down to them. Whether anything of a sermon rubs off on them or not, even at this level they function as a catalyst.

Our sermons are always preached at speed. I am not quite sure which came first, my rapid style of speech which forced a pattern on the congregation, or the type of congregation which moulded my speech. The kind of attention one is given does partly depend upon what is being said and how it is being said, but it also depends on the mood of the congregation when they arrive. Sometimes their mood can be affected by that of those taking the service. I have noticed that on those occasions when I have come to a service ill-prepared, my own resulting anxiety has communicated itself in a restless way to the youngsters. They have thrown me off my stroke many times, and thrown the congregation for that matter too, but sometimes the fault has been on my side. Thus we do learn the hard way the lesson that we belong to one another. I have often been guilty of feverishly trying to arrest their attention by fair means or foul. By this I do not mean standing on my head in the pulpit. Looking back over old sermons, I can honestly say that the means have not been deliberately foul although they have often been over-contrived. This does not mean to say I agree with the student visitor to the church who complained after one of my sermons that all the illustrations were much too local and might have given offence.

I suppose two types of preaching are in the main possible. First there is the sermon which begins with a text and which ensures that text is basic to the whole theme. It is also given a

modern application which is consonant with the correct interpretation of the text. A heavier example of this kind of sermon
consists of expounding a whole passage but also relating it.
The second type is thematic preaching where the preacher
begins with a theme or situation, usually an unbiblical one, but
relates it to a text or passage in a legitimate way. By legitimate
I mean not doing what many of us have been guilty of doing,
which is simply dragging in a text for decency's sake. In our
worst examples, many of us simply use a text to peg on a theme
or a theme to peg on a text.

I prefer the thematic approach simply because, in my experience, the announcement of a text or a reference to a biblical
incident brings about a shifting of feet, a searching for sweets
and ill-muffled groans. It means nothing, it cannot bring any
sort of action in its wake and, especially to the newcomer, it
confirms the belief that to be a Christian is to enter a realm
where a new language is a basic necessity for conviction. In this
kind of situational preaching the start has to be made with
what one hopes are everyday experiences of the people who
are gathered together.

This of course can have results never foreseen in the prepara-
tion. Once, when I had attempted to preach thematically on
turning the other cheek and had related it to the scriptural
injunction, an irate youngster came to see me the following
week. "I've tried it and it don't work." "What don't?", I said
unconsciously matching his idiom. "This . . . . business of
turning the other cheek. I've tried it." "How do you mean,
you've tried it?" "Well," he replied, "our old woman [his
mother] 'it me." "So?" "Well, she 'it me five times." "And
you just stood there?", I said. "Oh no," he said, "when she 'it
me the sixth time, I belted 'er in the teef." He had tried. But
the failure of his attempt had made him cynical about anything
said by those people who are supposed to be above contra-
diction.

If we who preach, as part of our attempt to present the total
claims of God in Jesus Christ on a man, are trying to communicate that the whole of life is part and parcel of God's world

37

and that every moment we are making a contribution for better or worse to that world by the way we treat it and the people in it, this is why illustrations, which to the outsider may seem trivial and are certainly unbiblical in the sense of not coming out of the pages of that unread best-seller, should be so much a part of the sermon. They are not dragged in just to make the whole thing come alive. They are there because they are themselves alive. You have to start where people are, and so the gospel should be in the illustrations because the illustrations are about normal people in their daily settings. It is not a question of 'this little story lets you see where God might be found', but rather one of showing that in that situation God is there already. As H. A. Dammers said, and has tried to put right, 'Christ spoke in parables and people fought for places: we talk of doctrines and religion and no one listens. Why?'[3]

We still tend to think that all we have to do is to talk of biblical parables and retell them. We hope that, if we do this, people will say to themselves, 'Ah yes, I know what this story says', and we hope that they will then go home happy. But this is not so. In our teaching we have bred nothing except perhaps less interest in the Bible, simply because we quote it without exposing ourselves sufficiently to its message before we pass it on. A second-rate sermon (of which I have composed my fair share) is often so second-rate because it is just a repetition of the second-hand stories which have no meaning for us and cannot have any meaning in action for the congregation. The young person who hears somebody start off with the story of the Good Samaritan is far more likely to think 'I've heard all this before. It didn't mean much then and so it's not likely to mean much now.' It is most unlikely that he will try to think behind the factual details to the attitude of mind which the story is attempting to convey. To realize this is basic to any attempt to communicate with young people, indeed people of any age.

The problem of the preacher, whatever his congregation, is to confront them with the claims of God in Jesus Christ. This

[3] A. H. Dammers in an Address.

includes the task of getting them to see that, preacher and congregation alike, they have their common responsibilities as the Body of Christ in the world. The preached word must contain the challenge to be the reconciling body.

This of course divides itself into the two tasks. One is that of an ambulance service to those not covered by the welfare state or even an extra pair of hands to the over-worked and under-staffed services as they are at the moment. The second is to help all who worship to see that the Church would still have a part to play in a society where none suffered and none were in need of meals on wheels or visitors to come just to listen to them. The Church cannot hope to survive into the twenty-first century as a sort of supplementary wodge of do-gooders. To have this view of life is to turn the ordinary man and woman in the pew into the sort of person C. S. Lewis devastatingly described as '. . . the sort of person who is always going about doing good to other people and you can tell the other people by their hunted look'.[4] We are not out on one big hunt to create the housing-estate equivalent of Graham Greene's leprophilic nun, 'But if we cure all the lepers, then what or whom shall we all look after?'[5] The need to look after those in need must be stressed, but not to the extent of creating the impression that the Church exists as the World Council of Churches exists – to do itself out of a job.

Truth can be taken only in very small doses, and preaching in a parish situation is a long-term process, greatly helped by personal continuity of ministry. To expect overnight miracles and conversions may be a kind of faith, but it is not realistic. Mark may have been badly muddled in his interpretation of the parable of the sower, but it must be admitted that some seed does take a very long time to produce fruit. Much of the fruit may be both unconscious in the mind of the doer and therefore unknown in the mind of the would-be sower.

True thematic preaching must be the result of good personal knowledge of one's congregation. H. H. Farmer wrote, 'To

---

4 Conversational remark attributed to C. S. Lewis.
5 Graham Greene, *A Burnt-out Case*, Heinemann, 1961.

succumb to the temptation to rely on your pulpit powers to make up for deficiency on the pastoral side is fatal. In the end it leads to what I can only call "French lacquer" preaching, bright and interesting, but lacking depth and tenderness and searching power. It takes on the brassiness which the Apostle said characterizes even the speech of angels when there is no love. You cannot love men from the pulpit. You can only love them in concrete personal situations wherein there is cost.'[6]

I have been asked to put down an example of the kind of sermon I am accustomed to preach. I do this with genuine trepidation:

There was a happening last week outside Mr Rowe's fish and chip shop. It was on Thursday night and our weekly dance had just ended. Some of those who had attended were having a delectable fish 'lot' of the variety that only Mr Rowe can supply (commercials in sermons, by the way, cost 10s a mention) when a short, sharp punch-up ensued. It was all over in a few moments. People resumed munching from their paper bags and eventually toddled off home. But the incident had been witnessed by a certain bus conductor and driver, and they had been appalled. Not that the fight had been too serious. What had shocked them was the language used by the by-standers. My housekeeper told me that the next day she was on a bus where the conductor who had witnessed these proceedings was recounting the story to a passenger. And he said this: "The language of those kids was appalling and disgusting, and do you know what? They had all come from that St James' Church Club."

Now this attitude of mind intrigues me, and we have had to put up with it in a variety of forms over the last years. I think it is a hypocritical attitude, but to that in a minute. We often see it when one of the church football teams is playing, and if I said one team in particular it won't take much guessing on your part to know to which one I am referring. Mr Phillips and I have often been in attendance at such matches on Saturdays whenever we don't have to take weddings and the like, and often we have stood there wearing our dog-collars. As soon as the match has got under way, we have given the occasional shout in support of our team, yelling helpful bits of advice like "You're half asleep, you dozy lot of nitwits!" or "Kids at kindergarten could do better!" and other delicate phrases designed to encourage the lads in their endeavours. Because of this, it becomes quite obvious to the opposing team's supporters that we belong to St James', which represents a quick bit of deduction on their part.

Now, lots of things happen in a football match, but I am only concerned tonight to mention one. Occasionally when lads, certain lads, get worked up or over-anxious or just keen, they say certain things which have not yet found their way into the Oxford Dictionary – though it would surprise you to know just what words have found their way into the Oxford Dictionary. Some lads can even spend almost the whole time using a vocabulary which has no parallel in the classroom or in the Sunday School class. Now, I am not attempting at the moment to go into the rights and wrongs of the use of such words. All I am stressing are the facts. Certains lads use certain words on the football field as well as off it.

What does intrigue me is the occasional reaction of the other side's supporters, especially if their team is losing, when they hear this language. They look at our collars, they hear the shouts for St James', they hear the words from our players, and very often march up to us, all of a tremble, and say "It's disgusting! A Church team as well!" And this seems to make them feel a little better, because they march back to their places where they continue to think inwardly the words which our boys were saying outwardly.

A bus conductor says "And do you know what, they had all come from that St James' Church Club" and your football opponent says "It's disgusting! A Church team as well!"

There are two points I want to make tonight as briefly as possible about this issue, and in giving our answer to such hypocrisy, because that's what it is, I don't want to get bogged down on the relatively minor point, 'Is it wrong to swear?' It might be better if certain words were not used, certainly in public conversation, but that's not the point. I have even been known myself to say certain words that perhaps as a Minister some would think I didn't oughter. For instance, when someone annoyed me intensely, or something has dropped on my big toe, before I could check it I have said "Bother!" and even "Drat!", which is pretty shocking, you must agree. So, as I say, I don't want to get bogged down on the rights and wrongs of swearing.

But the first point is this, and here I am afraid I cannot help but drag in the Gospel. In the Gospel lesson tonight, we read that passage which contains some of the collected sayings which denounce the hypocrisy of certain scribes and pharisees. At one stage, Jesus says 'What miserable frauds you are. You clean the outside of the cup and dish while the inside is full of greed and self-indulgence. Can't you see, pharisee, first wash the inside of the cup and then you can clean the outside.' And then in even stronger terms, '. . . you are like whitewashed tombs which look fine on the outside but inside are full of dead men's bones and all kinds of rottenness. For you appear like good men on the outside but inside you are a mass of pretence and wickedness.'

Now, this may be a rather strong way of describing a Lockleaze bus conductor and a handful of grotty spectators at a football match, and I don't want to spoil the point by over-exaggerating it. But there is a cap here which fits all of us. You see, when many of these people hold up their hands, often in mock horror at what they hear, they're basing their judgments of people on first impressions and on sometimes very superficial characteristics. When I first went in the army as a conscript – they wouldn't have got me any other way – until that time I suppose I had led a fairly sheltered life, been lucky enough to have a very good home where I never heard an angry word pass my father's mouth, never mind a swear word. Mother could get hopping mad occasionally, but her righteous anger never produced an expletive – a swear word – and I suppose I grew up thinking everybody talked and behaved as reasonably as that. So when I first went into the army I got quite a rude shock. And the thing that shocked me most of all was the language, and what I took to be filthy language, in which many of my comrades' seemingly indulged all the day long. And for long enough I made the fundamental mistake of judging them as persons by what they said. I tended to pick my friends from those who were 'nicer', if you see what I mean. But gradually I learnt a lesson. After all, you can't sleep in the same Nissen hut with thirty other blokes for three months' basic training without beginning to learn something about them as people. I gradually discovered that some of those blokes who swore and who didn't seem to care what they said, whose vocabulary seemed limited to a very few colourful words, had a warmth and depth of personality which was very attractive despite, and sometimes because of, the same colourful vocabulary. Some of them, I found to my naïve surprise, were more loyal in trouble, more encouraging amidst the general gloom of training life, more considerate towards my own failings, than some of the 'nicer' young men to whom swearing was as alien as the proverbial chalk from cheese. And of course this is precisely what Jesus kept on emphasizing, and is implied in those words we quoted. If you judge by outward appearances alone, then you're going to miss an awful lot of fun and warmth and love, whereas if you just take outward appearances as your standard, you could end up with some very poor friends indeed.

No, I am not making a strong plea in support of swearing outside Mr Rowe's fish and chip shop or on the football field – I am just reminding us not to be too quick off the mark with our condemnation – miserable lot that we can be.

And of course, to take this a little further, it was all very well for me in the army turning up my nose at those who swore, but looking back I could have hurt them more than they hurt me. I happened to have had a reasonable education; most of that intake had not. Many of them came from the rougher parts of Glasgow. In an argument or awkward situation in the barrack room, all they had as weapons, apart from their fists, were the

43

few amazing words that they flung around as fast as they could open their lips. I had a whole host of decent words at my disposal, but I also had the ability of putting lots of individual decent words into all sorts of harsh and bitter sentences that hurt much more than the tatty swear words that were flung back at me. So let's remember that when we condemn people for the words they use, our use of ordinary vocabulary can be a much greater sin than theirs if we so use our superior knowledge to hurt and keep on hurting.

And the second and last point I would make is this: all right, we agree, Mr bus conductor, Mr football spectator, Mr whoever you are, that you have happened to hear from time to time certain young people swear, and these very same young people go to SAINT James' Youth Club and play football for SAINT James' football teams. And it is quite possible that there are one or two naughty boys (and girls) amongst them. But so what? So blankety-what? What are we supposed to do about it? I would like to ask them three questions. 1. Do they think that we teach them to swear here? To put it at its most ridiculous but logical best, do they think at 10 o'clock on a Thursday at the end of a dance, I get hold of the microphone and say "Now remember, when you get over to Rowie's, let's have bags of mouth"? 2. All right, some of these kids do swear and a few are not very nice with it. Do they expect us to be able to work magic and prevent them swearing in the heat of the moment on a football pitch or outside a shop at night-time? We may well be our brother's keeper, but this is just ridiculous. And 3. Because they swear, should we ban them from the club and from a church team? If so, who's going to deal with them? It's this last point which I want to end with tonight.

St Paul said 'While we were yet sinners Christ died for us.' Jesus loves even the likes of you and me. He doesn't ask careful questions about us before he accepts us and does not demand that we should fulfil certain conditions first, before he dies for us. He came to people where they were, as they were, and he comes to us now while we are what we are, without asking conditional questions or demanding that we first take up respectable attitudes. We can ignore him, crucify him if you like, but he keeps on coming and loving, until he has won us for his Kingdom.

So do you see the hypocrisy of all this now? He is a fool, who says "And they go to St James" for he is showing his own ignorance of the Gospel. If it wasn't for the love and forgiveness of God, not one of us would be here tonight.

Don't let's ever forget that, especially when we are dealing with those people we don't like.

The preacher concludes the sermon with a bold amen, in which occasionally some of the congregation have joined. Whether they have participated out of a feeling of relief or no is not always clear. The Offering is then announced, and is taken as a separate part of the service, while the congregation remains seated. Conversation is inevitable during this operation, although not on the pre-service scale. From time to time a reminder is given that the Offering is an act of worship. The opportunity to relax enables the mustering of a second wind, bringing with it strength to last out the remaining moments and to concentrate with reasonable attention on the final hymn. As the Offering is carried up the aisle the congregation stands to sing 'Praise God from whom all blessings flow'. Thereafter the final hymn is announced. The reciprocal Blessing is then given again, 'The Lord be with you', 'And with you', followed by the Benediction, with the congregation remaining standing throughout. There is a momentary pause before the alms dish is returned to one of the deacons, who turns and walks down the aisle, hotly pursued by the Ministers, who in turn are hotly pursued by the congregation.

"I have never seen", said a visitor, "a church empty so fast. You would think they are relieved to get out." He didn't know how near the mark he was.

4

'Not on your Nelly'

THIS CHAPTER is devoted to a transcript of a tape-recorded conversation I had with two of the boys who, for a while, attended regularly on a Sunday evening, mainly, at first, because of the attraction of the club afterwards. They did not know that the conversation was being so recorded, but they have since given their permission for it to be printed. Indeed, there is nothing in it of which they are ashamed, and they feel it represents the views of many of their contemporaries.

The two boys in question are ordinary working lads, whose views on religion the regular churchgoer might dismiss as half-baked and ill-informed, but which nevertheless do represent the views and misconceptions of many people today, both young and old. And in any case, it is all very well for us to come over all superior and condemn them as half-baked. Whose fault is that?

In typing the transcript, I have missed out a few of my own linking remarks where it possibly could be done. Most of these consisted of the usual 'ha ha' or 'is that so' or 'you don't say' variety, and to write them down would simply detract from the main theme.

This conversation arose after the boys in question had told me that the school club to which they belonged had been visited by four lady evangelists, who had come to try to convert them.

You must not gather the impression that Bruce and David are a couple of delinquents. They had sized up their quarry pretty well and at times were simply testing their shockability.

MARVIN   What were they?

DAVID   Some was missionaries, the others was vicar's daughters.

BRUCE   They were wives, you know like.

MARVIN   How did you know they were vicar's wives?

DAVID   Well, she told me so, when I was chattin' to 'er, you know.

MARVIN   What did she say? She was a vicar's wife?

DAVID   Well, she said. I said to 'er, Well, wha'd you wanna be then, you know like, being a bit interesting, on what she was on about. So she says she always wann'ed to be a missionary, and the other one turns round and says, I always wants to be a vicar's wife.

MARVIN   Oh, she wasn't a vicar's wife? She wanted to be one?

BRUCE   Yeah.

MARVIN   Was she engaged to a vicar?

DAVID   I don't know. She was always on about it. That's what she told me. So I said, I'm a vicar's assistant – so try me! See. Just for a laugh.

MARVIN   Well, were they students? From a college?

BRUCE   I think they were.

DAVID   I don't know which college they come from. But I do know they was students, because a bloke called Mr Baker what runs the club told me so, you know. Anyway, first of all they come over to my girl-friend like, and ask 'er if she done any caving. So that's what started me off. I mean caving! Let's be fair about it.

MARVIN   Yes, let's.

DAVID   So she asked me, um, she goes, er, d'you do caving or anything like that? I says, Well no, I likes to have a little bit of old snog in the dark, things like that, you know. Well, you know how it is!

MARVIN   Do I?

DAVID   She says, Well, er, what d'you think of the club? Well, I says, it's hopeless. I don't like it at all over 'ere. She says, Well, why d'you come over 'ere? Well, I says, I got to

47

'ave sommunk to do on a night time, 'aven't I? Instead of going around beering, bashing coppers an' people and summit like that. She goes, What? she goes to me, she goes, I reckon I could convert you lot.

MARVIN Convert you?

DAVID Yeah, you know. Get us goin' to church an' all that. You go because you want to go, an' pray because you want to pray, an'——

BRUCE Sing.

DAVID Yeah, sing because we wanna sing. Then I said, Look, I said, our minister, Mr Marvin, been trying for years to do that, and 'e ain't succeeded. I said, If 'e can't do it in years, you won't be able to do it in months, weeks or years.

MARVIN You've got a point there.

DAVID I said, 'e tries thoroughly, I know, I said, I go to church. She said, Well, d'you go cause you wanna go? No, I said, I go cause I get in the club. That's right, ain't it, Bruce?

BRUCE Yeah.

DAVID So anyway, she goes to me, er, Why d'you go to church? So I said, Well, if I don't go to church I don't get in the club, I said, that's the way it goes like.

MARVIN That's the way it goes.

DAVID An' she said, Er, well, what d'you do when you get in the church? I says, Stands up, sits down, stands up an' walks out. She says, Well, what about singing and praying? So I says, I don't sing an' I don't pray. I just stands there an' sits, you know, an' that's it. Anyway, she said. But God loves you an' he expects you to speak to 'im, like yer girl friend loves you an' speaks to you an' expects you to speak to 'er.

MARVIN Oh yes, what did you say to that?

DAVID I said, Yeah, well, course she do. But 'ats different, ain't it? Be fair. She says, Ow is it? So I says, Well, it is. She's real. She says, Well, ain't God real? So I says, Look, lemme tell you summat. So she goes, What? I goes, Look. You was brought up to believe in it, warn't you? She goes, No. I goes, Course you was, I said. D'your mother make you go to

church when you was young? So she goes, Oh yeah. So I
goes, Well, there you are then, you was made to, being
brought up in that kind of religion, you was made to believe
in that kind of thing. She goes, Well, she goes, when I was
seventeen, I 'ad a message, God sent me a message, an' he
told me that this was the kind of thing I should do. I said to
'er, Well, I ain't got any message yet, an' I can't find a job,
cor, for over a month now. An' I dunno what she was yappin'
about all them different things an' the like.

MARVIN Did she say anything to you, Bruce?

BRUCE Yeah, she said, D'you believe in God? Well, I said,
I believe in God, but 'ow, sort of fing – well, 'ow d'you know
'e's there, if you know what I mean, 'cos 'e's supposed to be
up there, an' we never sees 'im in any form. An' she says,
Well, what about Jesus Christ, 'e died for us. I said, Yeah,
well, can you prove that, an' she said, Yeah. An' then she
went on about 'er bein' a missionary in Africa, an' 'ow she
was goin' to make 'em believe. An' she said they people that
don't believe got no hope. But I said, take your Chinese, who
believe in that Buddah or somefink, ain't it? You can't
blame 'em at all for not believing in 'im, I said, cause they
'aven't 'ad no chance to believe in Jesus. Only der Buddah.
I said, Well, don't you reckon they got any hope, then? An'
she said, no.

DAVID The thing what made me laugh the most was, she
said to me, she goes, Have you ever read the Bible? I said,
What d'you mean? She said, Well, sat down at home an'
read it. I said, No, I said, course I ain't, I said, I got better
things to do, ain't I? So she goes to me, What d'you mean,
better things to do. That's the best book in the world, she
goes, the Bible. So I says, So it might be, I says, I didn't say
it wasn't, did I? She says, Have you read it, like? So I said,
Well I 'ave read a bit of it. She goes, At 'ome? I says, No,
when I was at school, when I was made to. So I goes, I'm
not goin' now, out from this club, and after I've took me
girl 'ome, to start reading the Bible. I mean, that's common
sense, be fair. Well, whaddo I wan' to read the Bible for?

49

MARVIN What did she say to that?

DAVID She didn't, she just give me a dirty look.

MARVIN I'll bet she did.

BRUCE There was another in there. She comes up to I an'
I says to 'er, for a joke, to 'er, I says, I'm all right, I do sign-
writing for the Governmint. She goes, Ooh, where? I goes,
I goes to the labour exchange an' signs on every week. She
looked as if she could kill I.

DAVID She did straight.

MARVIN What else did she say? Did she talk about the
Passion Play?

DAVID Oh yeah. She says, Were you in the Passion Play
like? I goes, Um, course I was. You seed it? So she goes,
No. I goes, Well, I was one of the stars like in it. You know,
I performed in it an' everythink. So she goes, Oh, she goes,
What was it like? I said, It was all right. I didn't mind it,
like. I enjoyed it very much. Well, she said, Did it make
you . . . Did it help you in any way to believe, you know,
to help you? You know, to understand it more. Well, I said,
it did, yeah, it did, I said, because it was in my generation
an' I understand it more than having these blokes —— about
with the Bible. I mean, I don't understand that, meself. But
the Passion Play itself, it helped me to understand the Bible
more, yeah.

MARVIN Yes, well, you may have satisfied her on that, if
not on anything else.

DAVID Oh yeah, but I didn't satisfy 'er on the other things,
'specially when she goes, I reckon I'd be able to convert you
lot in a couple of weeks. I said, Not on your nelly. Anyway,
my mates, they won't go anywhere near 'er, like, they found
out what she's like, what she was, an' so they stayed their
distance.

BRUCE I got lumbered.

MARVIN You got lumbered with her, did you, Bruce?

BRUCE Yeah. Well, I reckon the sorts of people that
come round stuffin' religion down yer throat, they ought
to be crippled, I do straight. They be cranks, because she

seemed, every minute of 'er life, just to live it, an' make it live over an' over an' over again. Well, she kept on, well, preaching about 'ow she wanted to go out an' teach these Africans, out in Africa. Well, she reckoned that, if they didn't 'ave any belief, they ain't never 'ad much chance of going up into heaven. Well, that ain't their fault, is it? Well, people that died years ago, it ain't their fault 'cos they weren't taught about Jesus. I mean, you can't blame that on to them solely. Now.

MARVIN No, I agree.

BRUCE Then she goes, There's millions of people, she goes, you know what, there's millions of people in the world, in Africa, she goes, who don't understand, you know, a bit about the Bible, they've never 'eard of the name of Jesus. So I said, Well what, so what, 'ave you looked in the hall 'ere? She goes, Yeah. Well, I goes, 'alf of they 'ere 'aven't 'eard the name. So what? Try learning this lot. She didn't like that at all, you know. No. I know I was being saccastic, but it was needed. I mean, cause you don't wan' that kinda person coming round.

DAVID Like Bruce says, dropping religion down you all the time.

MARVIN And she knows you come to this church?

DAVID Oh yeah, cause she said to me, she says, Oh, she said, I've 'eard about Mr Marvin. Oh, I said, aye, 'e's a good vicar, ain't 'e.

MARVIN That's right!

DAVID He's one of the best in England.

MARVIN Hear hear!

DAVID Don't comment on yerself. But 'e's one of the best in England, you know, I said, they don't come no better. An' she said, Why? An' I said, Well, for one reason, I said, mostly 'e lets us do what we wanna do, you know, beyond reason, I said. I mean, you know, we can't go round bashing up everybody, or breaking the 'all or doing certain things, I said. If we do a thing wrong, an' 'e don't agree with it, 'e'll tell us so. But I mean 'e won't come round, telling us an'

preaching us all about God an' Jesus – 'e won't preach about
the Bible any time to us, unless we wants to, an' we turn
round an' say, Mr Marvin, would you tell us about it – which
we don't do. We never do that. The only time we ever hear
about the Bible is when we're in church. Which we do go to
on a Sunday, half of us up here in Lockleaze. I say the only
time we really hear about it is when we go church on a
Sunday. The half of us go. Well, what I mean is you won't
be able to get in the club if you don't go to church, so you
gotta go to church, 'aven't you?

MARVIN Didn't she say something to you about singing the
hymns?

BRUCE Oh, ah, she says to me, Don't you sing the hymns?

DAVID I said, What d'you mean, sing the hymns? I said,
course I don't. Well, she said, why not? So I said, Why
should I, I said, I mean. Mr Marvin, I said. Mr Marvin, 'e
said to us once, Look, 'e said to us in the pulpit, when 'e was
speaking once, 'e said, Look, I don't care if you lot sings, or
don't sing – 'cos you can't sing. Which is right. We can't sing.
So we might as well shut up. She said, I don't believe it. I
said, Look, I said, 'e told us hisself. Which was fair enough
with me, 'cos I can't sing. I mean, I can't sing an' I don't
wanna sing. There's nothing there that makes me in that
kinda power to sing, I mean, the only time I sing is when
I'm happy. An' I'm never 'appy when I go to church.

BRUCE I said to our Dad, I said to 'im one night, I said, it
was about six or seven months ago, I said, Dad, I'm goin' to
church. D'you know what 'e said? 'E turned round an' said
to me, What are they givin' away?

DAVID Now you get on wif it, Bruce.

BRUCE I went to a church out St George. Well, just when I
left me job down summer 'ouses, I went cause I promise me
mate I'd go out there like. He wanted me to see his girl an'
all that. I went in there, an' that preacher, 'e was goin'. 'E
looked up an' said that God was behind everyfink. An' I
thought I'd 'ave a go at 'im about that after like. So I got 'im
in a corner an' I asked 'im an' I said, Look, I don't agree

with 'ee. I said, You mean God's behind good? He said,
Yeah. An' 'e's behind everyfink? An' 'e said, Yeah. Are
you tellin' me God's behind evil then? An' 'e tried to explain
to me that in . . . in a . . . . in . . . in . . . er . . . an indirect
sense 'e is if you know what I mean. But I just can't see 'ow
'e is. Not if 'e's, not if 'e's, if 'e's . . . Such a good man as
they say.

DAVID The 'ole sense of it, about this woman what I'm
trying to get at is, this woman, I think 'erself was thinking,
if she was given a certain bit of time she'd be able – er . . .
to convert half the boys in Lockleaze . . . to go to church
cause they wanna go, pray cause they wanna pray . . . an'
sing cause they wanna sing. An' that's impossible cause they
don't sing, they don't pray an' they don't wanna go to church.
I mean, I told 'er straight. For she said, Ain't you got no
feeling for goin' to church? Ain't you got a kind of thing
inside you what makes you wanna go? I said, Well, I'd
never found it. Anyway, she went on an' on about certain
things, you know the kind of things, an' so when the time
comes, I seen old Bruce, an' I lumbered 'er with 'im.

BRUCE An' it wouldn't 'ave been so bad if they'd had a
couple of pretty 'uns in there. They'd gone all bad.

5

'A Man Dies'

CONVERSATIONS LIKE the one contained in the previous chapter have not been uncommon, and when you consider that Bruce and David had been present in church reasonably regularly for a period of two years, it is quite apparent that their participation was often only at the 'stand up, sit down, stand up, walk out' level. A hundred and four sermons, no matter how thematic, had not added overmuch to their religious education. Slowly we began to discover what I know must be self-evident to many more, that it is not even half the battle to get young people into church. When they poured through our doors, it was only the beginning of the problem.

One day in February 1959 I received a letter from Ralph Morton, Deputy Leader of the Iona Community. It was to say that a young actor from the Citizens' Theatre, Glasgow, had just landed a job at the Bristol Old Vic. He was an associate member of the Community, and as I was a member, Ralph Morton thought I might like to make contact. The young man in question was Ewan Hooper, who has since played leading roles with the Old Vic, on television and on films. He is now Director of the Greenwich Theatre Project which, after many years of endeavour, will soon be providing south-east London with an exciting new theatre. In a few years he has certainly come a long way, but in 1959 he was a little-known actor, although considered good enough to be appointed to a company of national and international repute. The Saturday after receiving the letter I booked for the Old Vic's performance of

Ben Jonson's *The Silent Woman*. Afterwards I went behind stage and introduced myself to Ewan. To my surprise, I found him a quiet, almost diffident young man, not at all what I imagined actors to be. The following Sunday he came to the evening service, and thereafter was a regular attender and eventually a member of St James'. When he and his wife departed for London, they left behind them many friends in the parish.

Ewan not only put up with the evening service but revelled in it. But he too became quickly aware that as a means of teaching about the faith and the Bible it was almost a total failure where the youngsters were concerned.

It was our custom to have supper together every Sunday after the youth club had finished, and usually the incidents of the evening were the main topic of conversation. We were never short of material. After one particularly successful Sunday night club, one of those nights on which everything had gone right from start to finish, we began to wax eloquent over the potential provided by the youngsters. The general sentiment expressed was: 'What can you do with such wonderful kids as those, youngsters full of vitality, capable of great loyalty, and responsive to us at a personal level, but for whom the Faith is a dead duck?' It was during the course of this conversation that we began to consider seriously if we could go any further in presenting to them the claims of the Christian faith.

We cannot remember whose idea it was, but suddenly we found ourselves discussing the possibility of writing a modern passion play in which the youngsters would participate. Of course, the hour was late and we had had a good evening, and I suppose that is why we continued to treat the idea reasonably seriously for the next hour or two. I am sure if it had occurred to us in the cold light of a Monday morning it would have been instantly dismissed. Looking back to those early days of *A Man Dies* in 1960, and thinking of the young people who made up the youth club, I am still not sure how the whole project got off the ground, but it did.

We did not have in mind what one normally thinks of as a passion play, that is, a re-enactment of the Gospel accounts as we think they actually happened. What we were thinking about was something akin to the medieval Mystery Plays, which, as far as we understood them, were performed in the dress of the day and in the language of the day, and were as much for the benefit of those taking part as for the audiences. They were acted for people who were unable to read and therefore could not read the Bible. Why not do something similar for people who could read the Bible but who saw no reason why they should? That was the theory anyhow.

We realized it was no use asking our boys and girls to take speaking parts, no matter how daring or modern the language might be. They simply would not have agreed to do it for they would have been too self-conscious. Therefore we had to look for a medium which they could use without embarrassment. What came to mind at once was their kind of music and dancing. Bill Haley had come to our shores in 1956, and by the end of the 50s skiffle was on the way out and rock 'n roll was on the way in. There have of course been many developments since, and for different productions of the passion play we have had to pay close attention to them. But in 1960 it was rock 'n roll. Could it be used as a basis for a modern passion play?

The idea that it could persisted. We would attempt to write a play which the young people would perform in their normal clothes and to a background of the music which they loved so much. The problem was how to convince them that this was something they would enjoy doing without being accused, in Bruce's phrase, of attempting to 'stuff religion down their throats'. We realized it would have to be 'sold' to them on the basis of 'We think it would be *fun* to do' and treat it simply as if it was going to be a chance for them to enjoy themselves. Even in those days we were not green enough to imagine that all we had to do was to gather the club together and say 'What fun! We're all going to take part in a passion play!' For one thing, the word 'passion' had other connotations for them, and for another, when the idea really penetrated, mob rule would have come into its own and it would have been quashed with utter derision.

But as we began to write a preliminary script, we became more and more excited by all the possibilities of the idea, even in the cold light of many a Monday morning, and finally we summoned up enough courage to tackle the youngsters themselves. And tackle them we did, but operating on the principle that where only two or three are gathered together we had more chance of winning the day.

I always remember the first group of five which I spirited away one evening from the youth club into the vestry. Hesitantly I mentioned what we had in mind and said I had gathered them, in particular, together because I hoped that, if we were to undertake the project, they might play leading roles in it. I was agreeably surprised that they did not laugh the whole thing out of court immediately. Indeed the atmosphere of a confidential *tête-à tête* with the Minister putting his cards on the table on a friend-to-friend basis seemed to rule out the possibility of any flippant rejoinders on their part. But they had many questions to ask before they were willing to commit themselves. What kind of role, Dorothy enquired, did I have in mind for her? I said I thought she would make an admirable Virgin Mary. At this, she frowned, paused, and then replied seriously: "But, Mr Marvin, I'm not a virgin." The boys, who seemed to be well acquainted with this fact, made no other response than to look at me to see what mine was. I mumbled that we were bound to expect little difficulties in casting and that they had to remember we were asking them to be actors and not the people themselves. But this was only a foretaste of what was to come.

For those who are unfamiliar with *A Man Dies* I would point out that it has grown enormously in scope compared with what was envisaged and presented in 1960. Details of its development will be touched upon in the next chapter. But for many reasons that first amateurish and improvised production stands out in my mind better than the subsequent ones which have admittedly been more sophisticated and, I presume to say, more professional.

A Man Dies has been labelled a gimmick by many people, but we would hotly deny this charge. It would have been a gimmick if we had attempted to impose it willy-nilly on a group of unsuspecting youngsters whom we hardly knew. But these were the kids with whom we had done battle in church and who were regular members of the youth club, and it was on a friend-to-friend basis that the suggestion was made. If we need any defence against the charge, it would be that, having endured the vicissitudes of our club life over the years, we were entitled to experiment in this way. The play grew out of the on-going situation.

Gradually, but not as slowly as we had expected, a large proportion of the club membership became excited by the idea.

Anyone who knows anything at all about a typical group of modern teenagers must at least recognize that the stage we had reached could have only been arrived at after long and painstaking attempts at communication.

So, I suppose, we saw some reward for the work of the past in that most of the youngsters who were approached on a personal level were quick to respond. That some of them saw it as a chance for a bit of a giggle there can be no gainsaying, but the majority, although not clear what we were about, were prepared to trust us.

But it was all very well having an earnest of their co-operation, but as yet there was no final script. Ewan and I began work to complete this at once. We kept very much in mind the idea of the Mystery Plays, in which not only was the Bible story re-enacted but there was also satire, humour and social comment. We were hoping to demonstrate that the Faith was concerned with the whole of life, and over the next few years, as it was added to and developed, this hope was basic to its whole conception. For instance, the attempt was made to show that the same sort of event that is described in the Exodus has happened in our life-time. Dunkirk was a miracle.

So was the deliverance of the Children of Israel. But the parallels were pushed further in an attempt to drive home the eternal recurrence of the same old problem and the sorry fact that we learn nothing from history except that we learn nothing. The glib phrases of Pharaoh were seen as in the mouth of a tired politician going through the standard ritual of saying nothing and giving nothing away on his return to London Airport. The frustration of the wilderness is mirrored in our frustrating existence as we chase the ephemeral gods of gurgling washing-machines and the like. During the crucifixion scene the words 'Father forgive them' were matched by a picture of the H-bomb being exploded on Hiroshima and by other examples of man's inhumanity to man. The failure of Joseph and Mary to find a room was turned into a scene common in our life today, that of colour-bar rejection. And so on all through the play.

We settled for a 'theatre in the round' presentation. In the first year, before we became more pretentious, we simply aimed to make use of our own church hall, which as church halls go is not too bad and had in fact been completed only two years previously. Technically it did not provide a complete circle for the audience, but we seated them around three sides of the hall, leaving floor space, as well as the stage, for the dancers and actors. A screen was erected above the stage, on which slides were projected, as a parallel to the acting in the body of the hall. In one corner of the stage we had the group, which consisted of a lead guitar, a rhythm guitar, drums and a tea-chest bass (shades of skiffle). This first year we only had one singer, a boy. Much of the action was described in song and dance, and the remainder was mimed to tape-recordings of dialogue and sound effects. A great reliance was placed upon spotlighting, and about a dozen youngsters were strapped precariously to various parts of the hall roof in order to operate the lights. The effect of all this in a medium-sized hall was, for some, quite overpowering.

In early 1960 we had no idea of the controversy that was about to break out. Besides the charges of resorting to gimmicks and blasphemy, another favourite one was that we were publicity-seekers. The only publicity we gave concerning the production of the play was in the local parish magazine. We simply announced that the members of the youth club at St James' would be performing a passion play at Easter. It would be a little different from the normal conception of a passion play in that it would be in modern dress and would be accompanied by modern music. The youngsters were enjoying rehearsals and would enjoy performing it at Easter. If nobody wished to come to see it, they would still enjoy doing it. But by the day after the publication of this news it was in several of the national newspapers, and by the end of the week it had received international notice. These articles and news items were usually entitled 'Rock 'n roll passion play in Church', 'Christ in jeans', 'Putting the Bible to Bop' and the like. It was taken up by television and radio, and for the next few weeks before production we were the object of attention from reporters and photographers. This certainly gave an added interest to the kids, but it did not have the effect that we feared it might have, of spoiling them and the whole project. They took the whole ballyhoo in their stride, and in the end, at the local level, we found it had not been altogether a bad thing despite the harm it did elsewhere. The youngsters recognized immediately how unfair many of the criticisms were, and they simply resolved to counter them in the only way they knew how, by giving as good a performance as they could.

The unsought publicity did, however, have an effect on Ewan Hooper and me. We just had to buckle down to the task of writing a script which would stand up to the criticism which was already beginning to come in from a variety of places. If it had not been for the wider notice taken of the play, I am sure we would not have spent so much time and care on what was originally meant to be a little, local experiment.

And so rehearsals began. A major problem was to retain the interest of the youngsters, and this could not have been done if rehearsals had been extended indefinitely into a distant future. Amongst the potential cast there was a large proportion of the type usually, and sometimes justifiably, thought of as having no staying-power. They can be too easily bored, and sometimes the demand to repeat a scene would be met with a point-blank refusal – nothing personal of course. So the whole play has been written very much with this problem in mind, and when analysed, it reveals a pattern in which the majority of the cast are called upon to dance certain crowd scenes and no more. The cues for such scenes are such that even the least intelligent can eventually be relied upon to respond without benefit of prompter. In the main the cast squat on the floor in front of the audience during their infrequent moments of inactivity.

Not even for our Albert Hall production four years later did we have more than twelve full rehearsals. Of course plenty of scenes were rehearsed with individuals and the musical and technical side involved much application. But provided all this was well prepared, there was no need to over-drive the rest.

In 1960 the unknown factor was: would these youngsters do it on the night? Many of those who witnessed the rehearsals, including Ewan and myself, had grave doubts on this point. Rehearsals were often wild; no other description is possible. We would rant and scream at them and they would rant and scream back. When they were not actually doing anything, there was nothing more natural than to wander around and chat to all and sundry. One of our theories had been that every rehearsal could be a Bible Class, but that pious hope soon disappeared after a couple of nights of yelling such requests as "Why didn't the Virgin Mary tell me she was going to night-school?" and "How long has Judas been in the pub?" When we stated, for the sake of our own health, that there would be a fifteen-minute interval, it was always at least forty-five minutes before they could be rounded up from various parts of the building and from the pubs. The second half of a rehearsal always took place with a truncated cast. We had doubts indeed. But even though some recent rehearsals have been as bad, we no longer worry too much about their behaviour at a public performance. Youngsters have a great sense of occasion, and the sight of that 1960 cast in performance moved deeply those people who had seen them in the raw at rehearsal and criticized them severely.

Rehearsals were kept to a minimum, and this has always been the case.

That performance of 1960 was played to a full church hall every night for a week and could have run for many more. But a week was more than enough for the youngsters, not to mention the harassed producers. Little did we know then that this was only a beginning.

6

'Never the Same Again'

FROM OUR first production until the Easter of 1966 *A Man Dies* occupied a great deal of time and effort. After the final performance in 1960, Ewan and I would have been only too pleased to have forgotten about it altogether, but we were not to be allowed to do so. We were surprised and overwhelmed by the insistence on the part of the youngsters themselves, as well as by many of those who had seen it, that it should be repeated. These requests did not abate when we got back to a more normal routine. By the end of the year we were constantly being asked by the original cast and by many others as well "When are you putting it on again?" This was usually accompanied by an urgent request, if not threat, that the enquirer should be included as a member of the cast.

We were now in the position of having potential volunteers in excess of the hall's capacity for actors and audience alike. It was through this pressure from below that we began to set our sights a little higher than the local scene. Finally, we succumbed to it and booked Bristol's Colston Hall for three nights in the spring of 1961.

The Colston Hall is the largest auditorium in the West Country and a very attractive one into the bargain. With the help of a sympathetic management we found now that we really had an enlarged theatre in the round, with room for a section of the audience in the choir stalls behind the stage. But the principle was the same as before, although the cast of well over a hundred was almost three times the size of that which took part in the first production. Even so we had a waiting list.

Again we played to capacity houses and, though there were times when we were in danger of biting off more than we could chew, a reasonably professional production was the result.

One of the features of the play has been its tendency to have a terrible dress rehearsal. That year's dress rehearsal at the Colston Hall was no exception to what was to be a constant hazard. Nothing went right. Long before the allotted time had run its course, our lighting operators were all at sea, and the main body of dancers seemed to be totally lost in the hall. The principal characters kept missing their entrances, and an inordinate time was spent trying to find them when they had lost themselves in the corridors outside. And of course the hall was in easy reach of at least sixteen public houses, which added to our problems. Ewan Hooper's professional integrity made him wish that we could finish the whole thing there and then. Instead the weekend was spent in tying up as many of the loose ends as possible, and that meant there was no sleep for several of us for the forty-eight hours prior to the opening night.

The first-night audience was packed in and the national press well represented. For a long time we had wondered if we should have the National Anthem at the beginning or not, but had decided against this. But in the event we wished that we had decided otherwise. If we had, we would have discovered before the house lights went down that the amplifiers were not working. The lights faded, the drum rolls began, the audience stopped nattering and rearranging themselves, but the drums continued to roll and roll and roll. There was no narration to be heard at all from the amplifiers, just a dull hissing sound.

Through the intercom I ordered the house lights to come on again. Ewan Hooper was, by this time, trying to get into the office of the sound engineer. Dashing upstairs and down he three times found himself in the cool night air, which he was in no condition to appreciate. He floundered in again, only to get lost in the endless corridors which led everywhere and nowhere as far as he was concerned.

Meanwhile I had more of a brainstorm than a brainwave

and shouted the first thing that came into my mind. Attempting to strike a note of authority, I announced over the public address system that unfortunately there were still some latecomers, and because of the nature of the performance they would not be permitted to enter, once it had begun, until the interval arrived. Would they please enter forthwith. This must have puzzled some, who could not see a spare seat anywhere, but what they could see was the cast in the corridors waiting to enter. "Come in," some called out, "someone has just said that there are some seats left." Luckily the cast did not respond. Then the fallible human being who was in charge of the tape recorders noticed that the volume knob had been turned down. He turned it up and *A Man Dies* was off.

Each production has had its share of similar close shaves and of near-catastrophe. It may seem to be of only domestic interest to mention such potential disasters but, if any of them had occurred, we should have been open to the criticism 'What can you expect from a bunch of amateurs, and church ones at that?' That they did not happen was due mainly to the foresight of Ewan Hooper, who gave to the production a professional touch which it could not otherwise have had.

The last night of that year's production was seen by representatives of ABC Television, who were sufficiently impressed to want a forty-five minute adaptation on television on Easter Sunday. This allowed two weeks' grace, two of the most hectic weeks I have ever spent. Not only did we have all the problems involved in transferring and adapting a stage production for the television medium, but we had to face up to a mounting crescendo of opposition on the part of many people who prejudged the whole enterprise as blasphemous.

Looking back on it all, the fuss and bother engendered on such a wide scale seems quite ludicrous, and I am sure could not possibly be repeated today, a short six years after. A highly misleading report of ABC's intentions was written up in the *Daily Express*, and from then on a great deal of energy was spent in trying to prevent *A Man Dies* being shown on television at all. The day before we were due to go to Birmingham for the production, my telephone rang so constantly for six hours that the selector switch at the exchange finally could not cope and the line broke down completely. That week a question was tabled in the House of Commons by five Members of Parliament in the hope that the play would be banned. The Independent Television Authority, which has a watching brief in these matters, engaged in much consultation with those who mattered and representatives came to Birmingham to sit in on rehearsals. Only an hour before the actual programme was due to appear was the final go-ahead given.

One of the reasons why it all seems ludicrous today is that, even to those of us who have been closely associated with the play, the film of that 1961 television performance is more of a period piece than anything else. But period piece or no, it has been in constant demand ever since and has been widely shown throughout the world.

The youngsters, however, as on previous occasions, took it all in their stride. Now there was the added excitement of a television studio. The only disadvantage they were to discover was that they were in the hands of professional producers and directors who worked harder than anyone they had known and expected a similar response from them. All the same, the adults who accompanied them kept close guard on the studio doors.

The following are examples of press reaction to the play, which simply illustrate the storm-in-a-teacup nature of all that had gone before.

Daily Mail It was a pity there should have been such a song and dance about ABC's rock 'n roll Passion Play, 'A Man Dies'. Advance protests on these occasions tend to give viewers a prejudiced attitude.

There is a tendency in this country to regard the unconventional as subversive. This attitude crops up from time to time when TV breaks out of its rut and tries something different.

Catholic Herald . . . this play was completely sincere and succeeded brilliantly in doing what it meant to.

I could not, for the life of me, find anything but praise for the originality and reverence of this production.

The Guardian   There was nothing in the controversial rock 'n roll Passion Play 'A Man Dies' to offend anyone except those who object to seeing the story of the Passion and Crucifixion in a contemporary setting.

Daily Mirror   ITV's modern play in the rock 'n roll idiom 'A Man Dies' made a brilliant production. ABC-TV were right to ignore earlier protests, for it was both moving and sincere.

'A Man Dies' made a brilliant production. It was for the Teen Age: Not everybody's cup of tea, with cigarette smoking and tousled haired disciples – Immature but still The Word.

Evening Standard   That rock 'n roll Passion Play: I'm glad it went on . . . isn't it possible that 'A Man Dies' has more cutting edge for them [*those to whom Christianity means nothing*] than the majestic services of Holy Week? (Dr Mervyn Stockwood – Bishop of Southwark).

Annunciation   This was humble in conception and devout in realization. Valerie Mountain's singing of 'Gentle Christ' had all the fresh devotion of a negro spiritual and I found it intensely moving.

The Evening News   . . . shocking? I don't think so, unless you rate rock 'n roll – and a hard look at mob violence – a sin. What mattered was that the message came over with humility and reverence.

Church of England Newspaper   . . . I don't think I shall ever think again of Judas Iscariot without seeing him jiving with a jeanager and explaining, 'I need the money; I need it honey'. I really felt I was seeing Judas for the first time.

Daily Telegraph   Although some viewers protested to Independent Television against the showing of the Passion

Play 'A Man Dies' last night, they were far outnumbered by viewers praising the production.

Daily Herald   ABC should be thanked for devoting their *Sunday Break* to this interesting experiment.

Daily Sketch   'A Man Dies' held my attention throughout. I am certain it had more chance of holding a teenage audience than any Passion Play ITV have offered yet.

The Universe   I found 'A Man Dies' one of the most moving Passion Plays I have ever seen.

At this stage we had a play which dealt with the passion narrative, starting with the events of Palm Sunday and ending with the Resurrection. ABC Television then approached us again to see if we could write something similar for Christmas. The result was *Man in Time*, which started with Moses and ended at the crib. For this occasion we took coach-loads of youngsters to Manchester, and again they acquitted themselves well, not without giving us some funny moments. Now we had the basis for a much longer play, and so it was that we prepared for an even more ambitious production at the Colston Hall at Easter 1962. The play was once again under the general umbrella title of *A Man Dies*, but it incorporated most of the material from *Man in Time*. We booked the Colston Hall for six nights, and except for the Easter Saturday night there were packed houses.

By this time we had almost literally lived and breathed the play for two years. We decided to give it and ourselves a rest. So, much to the dismay of many of the youngsters, no performance took place in 1963. However, a more ambitious idea was beginning to circulate amongst a few of us. This was to attempt a production at the Royal Albert Hall in London. The more we thought about this, the more there developed a love-hate relationship with it. Finally it did get the better of us, and contracts were signed for one of the few available nights left in the spring of 1964.

Then began what was almost akin to a military operation. Again details of the planning involved, publicity, coach-organizing, ticket-selling, the financial risk we had to run without benefit of backers, and all the rest, are more of domestic interest, but day and night for weeks they absorbed the attention of a whole host of people. Had we bitten off more than we could chew? If it is true to say that the youngsters were never perturbed by the problems of production, which they could see, they were certainly not affected by the host of administrative hazards that weighed down so many of their elders and which they could not see. The theory has always been that a project such as this helps to build up a fellowship. But at times its only merit seemed to be that of simply testing how much the fellowship could take without disintegrating altogether.

The 1964 production was an even more extended version. It continued into the Acts of the Apostles and ran for two-and-a-quarter hours. We also booked the Colston Hall for a four-night run, a fortnight before the London engagement. Before either of these productions, EMI recorded most of the songs on an L.P.[1] and the script was published by Darton, Longman and Todd.

In the Albert Hall the dance area was the whole of the arena, well known to Promenaders. Even the hundred or so of the cast we were accustomed to have performing at the Colston Hall would have been lost in that vast expanse, so now for the first time we were able to incorporate everybody who wished to be in the play. The final cast list included a hundred and twenty seniors and eighty juniors, not to mention forty technicians and ninety adult helpers. All these had to be taken to London from Bristol in the early morning, fed, and rehearsed in the afternoon in an unfamiliar building. They then had to perform in the evening to an audience of six thousand and return that night to Bristol. There were those who said we were driving them too hard and that at the very least we should have remained in London overnight. But by doing it this way

[1] No. 33SX 1609 in the Columbia Records series.

we stood an even chance of returning with at least ninety-five per cent of the cast. It was difficult enough to keep two hundred youngsters locked in the Albert Hall for almost eight hours until the performance began, knowing that if once they disappeared across the road into Hyde Park we might never find them again. As it was, with the labyrinth of corridors which engulfed the arena, sufficient of them went missing for various lengths of time to help the dress rehearsal to degenerate into what must have been one of the most disastrous on record at the Albert Hall.

ABC Television were present to film the whole of the play. For the previous fortnight they had been filming at St James' and in the youth club and they had cameras installed on the coaches from Bristol to London. The result of their endeavours was an hour and forty minute feature on Easter Sunday night. But after the dress rehearsal TV producers, adult helpers and the rest of us (apart from the cast) simply wished to crawl away and be forgotten.

Another hazard was that, because of union rules, the lighting had to be done by professionals. This, since it was their first introduction to the play, only added to the chaos. Reporters and photographers were present in large numbers and frequently became entangled with the cast at vital moments. By the time the arena had been cleared for the arrival of the audience, we had completed only Act II.

But the gods smiled, and although no one who knew the play from the inside was able to relax one bit during the performance, the overall result could not have been better. By this time we were very fortunate in the musicianship of the group and, above all, in the extraordinary talent of Valerie Mountain, our lead girl singer. Valerie has been in every production except the first. As a result of her work in the play, she was offered lucrative television contracts, but declined them all. As a member of St James' she has been of great assistance from time to time in the leading of the worship. She also sang the lead part in the film *Some People*, in which Kenneth More was the star.

The last public performance of *A Man Dies* by St James' took place at Easter 1966, and there it rests. It has been performed by many clubs and organizations in this country and in other parts of the world, and we hope it will be of use for some time to come. But it was written at a particular period and as time goes by will no longer have the relevance or the impact it once had. But we hope it has helped to give a lead and to show that in each generation appropriate vehicles for communicating the faith can be made available.

We are often asked what the play has done for those who took part in it. By this some people mean how many of the young people have been saved, or how many of them have become church members, or at the very least what changes has it brought about in their general attitude to life. The first two questions are more simply answered than the last. The facts are that out of a cast which over the years has amounted to several hundreds, only a dozen or so have become confirmed. They would probably have become such without participating in *A Man Dies*. When this is mentioned to certain enquirers, one detects a kind of 'I knew it' attitude, as if such facts proved all. But if *A Man Dies* had resulted in large-scale conversions and full communicants' classes, then it would have been proved to be the technique *par excellence*. In that case we would have been in duty bound to produce it twice a year.

In the light of this, some have said that it was a complete waste of time. If people think that the priority was to make church members, which seems implicit in so much that they have said, then it might well have been so. But I hope we have shown by now how limited an aim this can be – at least in one's initial relationships with those who are 'outside' the Church.

One thing that *A Man Dies* certainly did was to give the opportunity to a great number of youngsters to engage in a common project which required them to exercise qualities of discipline, loyalty and hard work, and in the process many of them discovered that they could enjoy exercising these qualities. Without attempting to play down the catastrophes and the

71

heart-searching that occurred from week to week, not to mention several relationships broken because of the play, the overall result was undoubtedly a deepening of a sense of fellowship amongst a group of young people who had hitherto been only loosely linked through their membership of the same club. This was to be a great help in the future whenever I found myself preaching about the Christian fellowship. I was able to illustrate from the play, its rehearsals and performances, to underline what were the duties and privileges of belonging to a true fellowship and how it differed from many groupings which go under that name. It has always been the hope that the sense of belonging, which many youngsters did experience while working for the play, could be transferred eventually within the larger context of the church. And although the vast majority of members of the cast have shown no inclination to become full members of the church, there have been many signs that they now look with affection upon the life of that church. This reaction demands from us in turn a long-term view and a continuity of pastoral ministry, not just from the ministers themselves but from all the church members. When from time to time we are able to visit some of these youngsters, most of whom are now scattered by marriage throughout various parts of the city, we know that a bridge-head has been established. Given more time and resources, I am convinced that the bridge-head could be a breakthrough. With present resources, to attempt to follow through with so many at a personal level is really to see how heavy the odds are against breaking even. But it could be done.

The play, however, did more than deepen a sense of fellowship among the young people taking part. It also helped to break down barriers amongst a wide cross-section of the life of the estate. Parents who never came near the church identified themselves with it in their support for the play against the prevailing opposition. Members of the cast were drawn into fierce disputes at their place of work and found themselves defending what they were about to do and having to search for reasons to back their defence. The church at least had become a talking point and, if you like, *A Man Dies* was in Bristol the poor man's *Honest to God*.

We are still discovering evidence to show that the play did help where the Bible was concerned. This is not the place to underline how closed and misunderstood this best-seller is, especially by young people. The interested reader can follow this up in the writings of Ronald Goldman and Harold Loukes. As David said, 'the thing that made me laugh the most was she said to me . . . "Have you ever read the Bible?" . . . I said, no, course I ain't, I said, I got better things to do, ain't I?' But despite this view many of the young people, including David, have a copy of the play and do read it from time to time. One or two others have told me how at night-time, in the privacy of their room, they act over again the parts that they played. The head of the Religious Education department of the local comprehensive school was fascinated to discover, when rehearsals were under way, how those pupils who were in the play had much better examination results than those who were not.

Although we certainly did not have it in mind when the play was first conceived, we soon found that taking a particular part could be a help to a boy or girl in their own personal lives. Modern psychology stresses the value of role-playing. This can take two forms. A person can either act out a role which bears a sharp resemblance to his own character or he can be cast in a role where the differences are equally sharp. The first method can help him to grow in self-awareness and to understand why it is that people react to him in the way they do. The second can help him to put himself in the place of people for whom he normally has little time and bring about a more tolerant attitude on his part towards them. This 'role reversal' put a boy of a usually quiet disposition into the shoes of a violent person and *vice versa*. No amount of talk could convince such opposites that there is something good and attractive in the other, but, since they had to act out the other's characteristics, it was possible to see developing a minute amount of understanding of the other as a person.

73

It was in ways such as these that *A Man Dies* can be said to have done something. The cynic may say that Cinderella on ice could have had the same effect. I would not agree. At the same time, if any church has enough initiative to cast scores of the youngsters around its doors in Cinderella, on or off ice, then it can never be the same church again and is bound to establish relationships which will stand it in good stead.

7

Brickbats

WHEREAS IT has been difficult to estimate the effect of the play on the young people who have taken part, it is not nearly as hard to discover how it has affected many a churchgoer – and for that matter many who do not go to church. Here are extracts from a few of the letters which we received from all over the world. I am not so naïve as to suppose that they are a fair sample of the reaction of the average man in the pew, but they are certainly representative of a section of opinion which at times is all too vociferous.

In the very first letter I opened, I read:

Since I saw you on TV, I shall not rest until I let you know your wicked smug smile nauseated me. When I read of your wicked play in the papers, I pictured an old senile man. What good can come to such wicked acting?

Fortunately not all the reactions to *A Man Dies* were of this sort, and many people have gone out of their way to say how moving and stimulating it had been for them. Others have been impressed by the complete absorption of the players in what they were doing. John Hale, who was then Director of the Bristol Old Vic Company and saw our very first production, said that what fascinated him more than anything else was that the young people taking part had no idea of the tremendous effect they were having on their audience.

Reviews in the press, when written by those who had been in front, have usually been favourable, often enthusiastic. News items written by journalists who have not seen the play have, not unnaturally, been written to make a 'story'.

The latter have sometimes misled readers, not least the five Members of Parliament, who announced their intention of tabling in the House of Commons a motion of protest against what seemed to them, at second hand, to be a piece of sacrilege. This came to nothing. The later intervention of the office of the Lord Chamberlain did, however, have an interesting result the rescinding of the regulation which forbade the portrayal of Jesus Christ in a public performance on the stage.

But to return to the letters, and first to some of those which were definitely abusive in their tone. They were, on the whole, the most interesting:

> How dare you call yourself a minister when you openly violate the Almighty in such a disgusting manner? . . . Take care, the devil is very powerful at the moment and you will be struck down by Michael the Archangel for your wickedness. . . . If I had my way I would make you be mocked and whipped until you called for mercy. . . . Take that Roman collar off at once, you Judas.
>
> Signed, one who is furious. . . .

And again:

> I think that you ought to be hung up by the heels and horse-whipped. At least you should be kicked out of the pulpit. Do you wonder that the churches are empty, when we have ministers such as you? Judas himself could not have done, and did not do, anything worse than you have done.

I doubt whether this was an attempt to whitewash Judas. I am glad too that writers of such letters did not see fit themselves to administer what they declared to be my deserts. It was odd that our play should have aroused a sadistic venom in people who presumably claimed to worship a God of Love.

Other critics, no less mordant in their tone, did not call down physical retribution:

> My thought is: – that with your Power and Love – you can do no more for our young people than these inanities then you at best, better seek another vocation. . . . Signed by a Psychiatric Nurse.

Nurse does not express herself with great clarity, perhaps because her psyche was gravely disturbed by our activities.

A correspondent from New York seems also to have let his words tumble over each other in his rage:

It is disgraceful, and you should be publickly censured and removed from your Church and be severely dealt with from the heads of the Church. To treat such a sacred incident in the life of Jesus Christ is infamous.

He does not say *how* he thought we had treated the incident. Perhaps this was because he had not seen a performance.

A writer from Michigan, another who had only read about the play, called up his reserves of contempt:

Dear Clown,
The newspaper carried the story that no one offered a word of criticism in reference to your irreverent comedy applied to a Christian service. Permit me to offer something. I think that you are an idiot. The backwash of the Reformation has brought incongruous parts and patterns. Yours surely must be the final dreg. 'Forgive them for they know not what they do.'

The backwash of the Reformation is a fine, resounding phrase, but I do not think we should hide behind the voluminous garments of Knox and Calvin. Indeed I wonder whether they would have approved of our enterprise any more than this critic from Michigan who seems to hold them and their work in such disrepute. We had of course hoped that we were not the backwash of anything but were rather doing our own stirring of waters which had become sluggish.

So far, I have quoted only those who attacked on a broad front. It has, however, been quite interesting to dissect the letters in order to find specific reasons why *A Man Dies* gave offence.

The first is the idea of Christ in blue jeans. This conception made a number of people hot under their (presumably) nonclerical collars:

I call it scandalous to put our Saviour and his Disciples in such a dress. Would they learn anything from it, anything Holy from such a play?

77

The second sentence, of course, begs a very big question. It is, however, irrelevant to our present process of dissection.

I have never read such a mockery to Christ before. Christ did not wear jeans but a beautiful gown and sandals on his feet.

One wonders if Jesus would have regarded his clothing as 'a beautiful gown'.

I write to express my very deep disgust and distress to think that a Vicar of a Presbyterian Church can so condone and lower his dignity by allowing such irreverence as you intend to happen. How can you put on a play which has a boy of nineteen (and a rock and roll singer at that) portraying Jesus Christ in jeans and a sloppy jersey? How utterly disgraceful. Do you think that our Lord, if he was on earth, would dress like that? It is nothing but a desecration and a mockery, and you, calling yourself a leader, should be the first to condemn it.

Jesus was not, of course, played by a rock 'n roll singer and the part was acted entirely in mime. It would be interesting to know what the writer considers the normal dress of a young carpenter today.

Surely no one can portray the part of God's Son, especially wearing a sweat shirt and blue jeans.

The portrayal of Jesus in any medium is inevitably a challenge which cannot be adequately met. You can't win. Nobody has – and this goes for some pretty notable artists of all kinds. Some of the greatest failures have been half-hearted attempts to recreate him as he was.

But the really big objection was to the use of rock 'n roll music, as it was then called, and dancing, which we had deliberately chosen as the idiom in which our youngsters could best express themselves and their feelings.

Another correspondent from New York wrote:

I have observed 'Rock and Roll' singers and dancers more than once, and if you believe that their gyrations and howls have a spiritual connotation, please show me how to interpret it in the future! I believe that God and his teachings should be taught as he wished, not by teenage howls and burps, but by sermon, lecture and question. I am sure he did not intend that his teachings would be compromised so as to lure interest by a floor-show. Your parishioners should conform to your way of teaching, not you to their whims!

One thing I cannot foresee is the subjugation of the Church to 'Rock and Roll' in the light of the teaching of the scriptures. It is certainly right to be progressive, but you have stretched the point somewhat. I have lived with the same situation here as far as that ludicrous form of dancing is concerned and have seen no visible results other than delinquency! I hope that your approach won't make the Church another 'jam session' for the already addle-brained teen-ager!

There is more food for thought in this than in many of the letters. I still believe that, even though we may have stretched the point a little, he has missed it. Our play did not extol rock 'n roll music and dancing, it merely made use of them for purposes of interpretation.

It was by no means the older people only who took exception to the music and dancing. Three letters written by teenagers are interesting. They draw attention to the fallacy of using the word 'teenager' as a rather derogatory title for an age-group, all of whose members may be expected to think alike:

Here is your 161st letter of indignation at your blasphemous 'Passion Play' – from a teenager this time. It is absurd nonsense which will do a great deal of harm. Imagine people actually laughing as the tragic story is unfolded. Rock and Roll should certainly not be introduced into this play. How can you dream of having God himself dressed as a creature [*sic*]? The meaning of the Gospels is lost completely in this stupid play and it will *not* be at all effective. I hope your bishop takes action. You should examine your conscience thoroughly. . . .

P.S. Conventional Churchiness? Follow Our Lord's convention and you will not go wrong.

I myself am still in my teens and I was appalled to read the other day that you are allowing the play, *A Man Dies*, to be performed in Bristol; not only that but possibly as a film for commercial exploitation around the sacred period of Easter. It appears that *you* have written this sacrilegious trash, in conjunction with Ewan Hooper; I would have thought that you might have known better. Have you a twisted, perverted mind also? Your sincere expression! 'One of its big moments is the arrival of Christ played by Mr K. Maughan, 21 years, who is greeted with shouts of yeah yeah and a rock 'n roll song instead of the customary Hallelujah.'

I don't feel that somehow this is the way to 'get through to these kids'. That disease spreads amongst us quickly and many of us are gullible and wishing to do something new. I feel that it's very wrong, not only that but blasphemous. This play brings you low in my estimations and I'm sure in all clean thinking people. Don't do it for our sakes.

I have just seen the Passion Play of Christ acted in 'modern' form on the television and I was disgusted by your reproduction of it. How you could dance and play beat music to such a sacred event as Christ's Passion amazes me. You can't possibly change a matter that happened 2,000 years ago into modern ideals without losing the original meaning, and that is just what you have done. Anybody with the minimum of intelligence can understand the story of Calvary, as it is written in the Gospels, without lowering it to pop music standards, so it was really rather unnecessary. Your play left no impression on my mind other than disgust. I am no 'square' and I am not writing against pop music, but you must surely see that the Passion of Christ is a sacred event and should be kept sacred.

So we stood condemned by some of the young people for whom we were trying to do something constructive.

One writer sardonically suggested that we might have gone still further along our sacrilegious path:

Sir, why didn't you . . . introduce the Twist in Sunday evening's orgy? It would have personified the mental condition of the long-haired philistines who took part in it and at the same time conveyed a message to the uninformed of what Christianity is all about, and given them a shrewd idea of what took place some 2,000 years ago.

Another letter contains two profoundly true statements. 'Jesus was not a rock and roll artist. He was the Lamb of God.' Nobody would dispute this. The letter goes on: 'I like to stay as I am; and Jesus did not want rock and roll or anything like that mockery at a time like that.' Here the meaning is less clear.

One splendidly abusive writer produced the following:

I understand that you are responsible for the disgusting rag put on ITV last night to oblige the non-believing youth of today, so as to mock our simple faith by allowing some layabouts and their girl-friends to parody the Crucifixion of Our Lord. I suppose that for you TWTWTW was not sufficiently nasty, so you would add the madness in your heart and head to add another disgusting episode in ridiculing religion on TV. I wish to God I could have been there to throw something at that moaning minnie yelling at the mike and beat away the scruffy layabout mocking Christ by his sordid mind. The world is rent by rock and roll so-called music and young people are passing back to the jungle. The beat to which they twist their bodies and their minds is approved of by infidels such as you. You have debased the Cloth. Are not gentle hymns and the normal service acceptable to you and your ilk, you masquerader?

The last words about rock 'n roll must be these:

I am sure that Our Lord's Mother did not like dances.

Of course, these two ideas, Christ in jeans and rock 'n roll music, were basic concepts. *A Man Dies* could not have existed without them. If they were wrong in themselves, then the whole thing was wrong.

A letter from the United States, calmer in tone than some of the others, shows that readers of reports of the play did not always jump to conclusions:

We are writing to you to inquire about the article, *A Man Dies,* which appeared in our local paper, March 28th 1961. The article caused a great deal of discussion in our senior English class. Most of the students feel that it is sacrilegious, but before we decide how we feel about this play, we need more information on which to base our opinion.

We feel that there must be a purpose in presenting the play in this manner and we would like to have further information, because it has aroused a great deal of interest in our class. We would be glad to reimburse you for any expense involved.

But not all were prepared to reserve judgment. Many felt that the old, old story and the old, old words were good enough:

Surely you can teach your young people to appreciate dignity, good music and the matchless English of Cranmer in the Book of Common Prayer without these vulgar stunts. You will never get people to respect Religion or even be interested, when it is presented in this blasphemous bad taste.

It is sad but true that dignity, good music and matchless English are not concepts through which one can work in the setting of the modern housing estate. It would be a privilege to hear Cranmer preach in my church, but whether he would be appreciated or not is open to question.

The next writer is again more sure of himself than many of us:

The whole thing was just making a fool of Christ and the Scriptures of the Bible. I should like to abolish all dancing on Sunday and have scripture reading and questions answered and a few hymns and some prayers. I am not altogether a Christian but I know when things are right or wrong.

Some took the line that Christ would not have behaved in this way:

We were disgusted and horrified at the so-called Passion Play in Modern Times. There is enough lack of Religion without you making things worse. These teddy boys aping when they know nothing about the life of Christ. The youth who stood and smoked a cigarette for a very long time as Peter. Then we had the usual savage shaking (so-called dancing). We had Judas, if you please, shaking hands with Our Blessed Lord. Then a teddy walking about with something like a chalice. I never saw such hypocrisy and complete ignorance of Christianity. Who on earth made up all this travesty? Blasphemy is the word for it.

Should Peter have smoked a pipe? One wonders what would have been said if the play had followed the Gospel account and made Judas betray the Son of Man with a kiss.

There were those who took the chance to identify our work with that of Satan:

It would seem that the idea is to entertain the Devil, not to fight him, and I think that strong words are needed in this day and age to speak up for what is right.

So do we.

And 'Disgusted American' seems to identify us with anti-clericalism at the least:

I believe you are sacrilegious! The very idea is sacrilegious! You of all people should know what Christ and the Crucifixion mean to Christians. The Son of God is far from being a Beatnik. What are you trying to put over to Christians in this portrayal? Do you think that God approves? The idea of the Church is based on God and his Son. Would you have people believe that he is a delinquent?

For the life of me I cannot see why he should suppose that I would.

So many people seem to feel that the Church and the world should be kept apart:

I do feel in my heart it is all wrong the way you put over our Lord's Death. What are you trying to do with our Lord's Death? I do think that you are trying to bring the things of the world into the Church. . . .

And again:

Please do not think that I am rude to write to you in this way. But to think of a Minister of the Gospel of Our Lord and Saviour mixing the Worldly things with the most sacred day of the year is appalling. We have had lots of young people won from these things and we don't want them to go back into the paths of Sin. If they read of your play, they will think there is no harm in this music and dances. But Jesus has told us plainly, 'Come ye out from among them'. All the way through the Bible I have never read that there was music around the Cross.

More briefly, if ungrammatically:

Did Jesus use this method? No, and he tells us plainly that we must come out and be ye separate.

It seems to be widely assumed that if the Church comes out into the street, it must necessarily grovel in the gutter. It is immediately accused of pampering to the Teds, Rockers, Mods or whatever the current name may be:

. . . You seem to have no time for the many decent, clean cut, wholesome types of teenager, who will spend hours at choir practice and could perform the Passion Play with reverence and sincerity. It is all too tragic that you laud the others to the skies, thereby increasing their vanity.

I have just seen a Passion Play performed by school children and it was beautiful in its honesty and sincerity. I should have liked you to have seen it.

One of the best of the 'anti' letters provided some material for the first public performances of the play in the Colston Hall, Bristol:

I refer to the photograph which has appeared in the *News Chronicle*. I find it completely distasteful. Why cannot these twitching and twisting teenagers sacrifice a little of their time in accepting the simple sincerity of a Church service as it is? Why should it be adapted to them? Teenagers have been placed on a pedestal by the back-room boys of the entertainment industry and the cheap press, who are cashing in on them as hard as they can go – Americanizing them and preaching to them that they are suffering from more frustrations than any former generation of young folks have had to endure. There has never been a time when young people had such a scope for entertainment and the money to indulge in it. Yet, they mill around, dressing absurdly and behaving rebelliously. And the Church has to try to meet them on their own ground. I will have none of it. I attended a country chapel service last Sunday and one of its members said to me, 'I would welcome heartily some young people dropping in here and accepting the form of simple service which was good enough for our fathers and their grandfathers. But I will never tolerate their bringing to these premises their American tunes and their American fashions.'

And here, before we leave the teenagers, is one of several letters from people who must be unable to get BBC or are compulsive viewers:

Once again it has been my misfortune to look and listen to your play and I suggest that you discontinue endeavouring to drag Jesus Christ down to the level of the teenagers, but instead try to lift them up to him. It is a good thing for you that I do not swear, for if I did then I would tell you exactly what I think of you.

It is sad that he should be unable to express strong views without profanity.

It was evident that some writers could find no one to disagree with them:

The music, words and acting were dreadful. Several people have said to me today, 'Did you see that awful thing on TV? Wasn't it terrible?' I can tell you it left me saying 'How long, Lord, must we have such things inflicted upon us?' . . . Please do a passion play but make it beautiful as we have always been taught by the church to believe that it was really.

Many of those who wrote assumed that the play was devised and produced as a means of attracting people, and especially young people, to church. As I explained in the previous chapter, this was not the intention at all.

What a disgusting mockery of Our Blessed Lord's death. If I were in your position and that was the only way I could get teenagers to church, then I should be pleased for them to stay away.

And so again, this time from the armed forces:

Apparently that is the only way you can attract your teenagers to church, by making a gimmick out of religion. Thank goodness I am a Roman Catholic, and that my Church does not need to stoop to this cheap and vulgar exhibitionism to attract converts to its Church.

So much for any ecumenical hopes we may have had, though, to be fair, we have had a very good press in several Roman Catholic publications.

85

The receipt of many letters from different parts of the world was indicative of a danger we had not foreseen, and perhaps could not have avoided, when the play was transferred from the domestic atmosphere of our own hall and presented to a worldwide television audience. A letter from Mexico, enclosing a cutting, makes a point which could never have arisen if the play had not emerged from its birthplace:

My reason for writing is to tell you that indirectly your new system has affected our Christian work here. We are trying to start a Presbyterian Church in the city of Puebla, and the most important newspaper has used your experiment against us. Their headline, 'To be sacrilegious it is necessary to be a Protestant', of course does not help us much in our work over here. I hope that you know enough Spanish to discover the ill intention of the author of the article, and the importance of a notice of such kind for all the Christian Protestant people working here. Of course you cannot well understand our religious problems in Latin America as you live in a basically Protestant country.

Would it be possible for you to let me know something more about this work that you are doing, explaining your point of view? It would help us much. Please forgive me, but I thought I ought to let you know about this matter.

It is certainly food for thought that our attempts to solve the problems of Lockleaze should have created difficulties for colleagues in Mexico.

The brickbats have been thrown from far and wide and for a variety of reasons. Some of them have hit the target. This is hardly surprising since the target itself represents no more than experiment, an attempt to break through. There were also many who, believing that a break-through might have been achieved, did us the honour of bouquets rather than brickbats. For these we were grateful, not least to this one:

I am an old lady (74) and pretty hardened and often critical in Church matters, but as I watched *A Man Dies* I was literally moved to tears, and I cannot thank you enough for that revealing play. There is a kind of 'purity' about the whole performance, done with such touching earnestness. And your conception of the contrast between the Rock and Roll callousness at the beginning and the joyous (still R & R) certainty of 'You don't have to go it alone' at the end is inspiration at its highest. I have been a communicant member of the church all my life, but this play brought more reality into my spiritual life than any of the thousand sermons that I have heard. Thank you again, and God bless your work. I am not signing my name in case you want to use my words to answer any criticisms (although I cannot see any possible cause for criticism).

Yours, Grateful Old Lady

The last words must be those of two postcards, both from the same address in Oxford:

24th March 1961

Re *Daily Mail* account of your proposed Sunday Play; how awful! Have you remembered that Christ, as well as being human, is also God Almighty? Do please read again Psalm 29.2 and Galatians 6.7 – also Hebrews 12.28 and 29.

From one who is the son and grandson of Presbyterian Ministers.

And then, dated 29.3.61:

Please forgive my previous p.c. written too hastily on the strength of a newspaper report of your teenage play. Having seen part of it on TV, it is difficult to understand the spirit underlying such a travesty of the production. I am sorry I did not see it all. Will you allow me to wish you all success in your efforts to catch the young imagination. It is indeed time that a little more should be used by the Church in the spirit of sincerity and understanding shown by you.

So we made one convert. We need his good wishes.

8

Hit First, Miss Later

EVERY YOUTH club leader has to face certain occupational hazards which at the same time constitute an opportunity and challenge. One such hazard and challenge is that provided by the boy or girl whom society frequently labels 'troublemaker'. We have had our fair share of them and often have succumbed to the temptation to wish that they would give us a wide berth. They can disrupt an evening simply by being present and can scare away half of your membership and make life uncomfortable for the rest. But to ban such youngsters from our clubs, although it may be necessary and wise in certain situations, is precisely to debar those who can benefit most from being accepted by a community. Of course it depends on the strength of this community and the quality of adult leadership there. But many youth club leaders have found that even the most recalcitrant boy or girl can be helped if he discovers a group which is prepared to accept him as he is without laying down preconditions of membership.

But this can be exacting work and can depend on adequate adult help and a large club membership within which the few 'hard cases' have no chance to take the centre of the stage. Once you have accepted in principle that they should be allowed to be present, then putting the principle into practice can have all manner of ramifications extending far beyond the context of the youth club. What follows in this chapter and the next may provide some indication of what these ramifications are.

'The last time I was hit on the head in London . . .

The speaker was a friend of mine, past middle age, whose position in life, one of respectable distinction, is remote from violence. Moreover he is an affable fellow, not liable to resort to his fists nor, I should have thought, likely to provoke others to assault. Nevertheless he has twice been attacked, apparently for no reason – not even robbery. Nor has this happened in the notorious alleyways of Soho, but in well-known, well-lit streets.

The fact is that violence has become a cult. It is all too easy to blame television, the paperbacks and the (mis-named) comics, writers from Micky Spillane to Ian Fleming, and programmes such as 'The Man from U.N.C.L.E.' and 'The Avengers'.

It is true that these are evidence of the cult, even its priesthood. It is true also that in the quick-to-read literature of an earlier day violence and cruelty were the prerogative of the villains, Fu-Man-Chu, Moriarty, Carl Peterson and their like. In such books the heroes stood for chivalry of a sort. They resorted to violence only as the sole means of foiling it in desperate circumstances by fighting wickedness with its own weapons. This applies even to Bull-Dog Drummond, acclaimed by some sociologists as the precursor of Fascism.

Now, however, the hero must be the toughest of all and reveal his toughness in violence for its own sake. This is the era of the anti-hero.

Nevertheless these are no more than emanations of something which lies deeper. The writers did not create the cult. They have simply cashed in on it. Gangster films did not create gang warfare. They revealed it. Edward G. Robinson played Al Capone. He did not invent him.

Fascism may be partly to blame. It is not without significance that the Rockers adopted a part of the uniform of the followers of Moseley. There is no denying that the young, however much they may claim to be individuals, like a uniform of a sort, one of their own choice, be it said. For a time the Scout Movement provided it, but for many young people in an increasingly sophisticated age it has clung far too long to its out-moded mumbo-jumbo. Kipling is not for today – not by a long chalk. Fascism, Nazism, and above all the Second World War provided the uniform. And the war, the first hundred per cent copper-bottomed, professional war in the world's history, sounded the death-knell of amateur, pseudo-chivalrous fighting. It produced its heroes, of course, but for the first time men, women too, were trained for what an earlier age would have called dirty fighting. There were no rules. No holds were barred. The war had to be won.

Our youngsters never knew the war. They have not experienced at first hand the good qualities which it engendered: courage, endurance, cheerfulness in adversity. They were born into a world in which there were many who had been trained to hate, to hit below the belt, to strike in the dark and from behind.

For us, too, in the midst of explosions, sirens, gun-fire and screams of pain, it was easy to believe in nothing at all, except that the prize went not merely to the strong but to the man who used his strength.

Those who censure the conduct of youngsters like ours in Lockleaze are too seldom ready to consider how far their generation is to blame for the misdemeanours of the young. It is a truism that young people will follow the example of their elders. And the biggest failing of the older generation has been the abandonment of parental authority, a retreat from responsibility which amounts almost to fear of one's children.

Parental authority does not mean waving a big stick. When they are quite young, children can be taught to accept the benevolent despotism of the parent. Authority which is blended with affection need not lead to rebellion.

Schools may be partly to blame too, but no school can establish a proper discipline without parental co-operation. There are far too many Mums who, having heard only one side of the story, will try to shelter errant children from punishment, not even listening to the other side, even when they hear it.

This will not prevent them, still more their menfolk, from giving a child a clip over the ear at home, without any consideration of justice. And so the child learns how to play off school against parent and *vice versa,* a habit easy to acquire, a trick which the young can perform with poker-faced skill.

Authority goes by the board. Impulse and an eye to the main chance take its place. You learn to hit first.

In general there are three main reactions to this state of affairs. One is passive, a sort of withdrawal of the skirts. This is a deplorable attitude. 'It is not my fault and I cannot do anything about it. I cannot understand it and I am not prepared to try.' Another is to bluster. 'Bring back the lash!' 'These young ruffians ought to be horsewhipped!' 'What is needed is more discipline.' The third reaction is starry-eyed. 'These poor kids have not had a fair chance.' True enough. 'They are only trying to express themselves.' True enough. 'They'll learn sense in time.'

Will they?

None of these reactions gets us any further. Mere persecution has never, in the whole course of history, solved any problem or achieved its purpose. And the sentimentalists ignore the plain facts of a situation which is hideously wrong. Right now the meek are not inheriting the earth. It solves no problems to invent cosy synonyms for sin.

So it is that the facts have to be faced by the Law and the Church, the copper and the parson.

The great thing about the old-style English bobby, the man on the beat in days when pressures were less exacting, was that he had a pastoral relationship with his neighbourhood. Probably he lived on his beat. Moreover there was, in those days, less emigration for work and for play from one neighbourhood to another. This was particularly true of villages, but applied also to working-class areas. In our days, with increasing and inevitable mobility of people, a whole city is a parish. There is so much more public transport. So many more people, young people in particular, possess their own means of transport – cars, motor-bikes and the rest.

The under-manning and inadequate payment of the police force adds to the difficulties. There are not enough happy policemen. They all have too many problems.

The result of all this is that the policeman does not have the same personal knowledge of his people that his predecessors could have. It is not his fault. His time is taken up with the detection of crime. There is none to spare for its prevention.

In this chapter we are not considering the big-time boys, the hardened criminals. This would need a specialized review from a better-qualified pen, and there are several. Our concern is the relationship of the Law and the young, the conditions in which petty criminals are born. Some of them graduate to the big-time stuff. By then it's too late for the local community to help.

I certainly believe the local community could help more than it does, but the problem is how to convince the local community that the naughty boys and girls are its responsibility. That is quite a problem.

At 6 a.m. a boy calls on his Minister. He comes because he knows his Minister and the Minister knows him. There is a pastoral relationship, a degree of mutual trust, some slight break-through.

He wants to tell me something in absolute confidence. Can he be sure that it will go no further? I say that he can be, taking his confidence to be at the level of the Confessional.

This actually happened five years ago. Perhaps now one would tackle the situation more wisely. But the point of the story remains.

Out comes his tale. He had been to a party. He got drunk. The youngsters were tired of the available records, so they broke into the local community centre, of which the boy was a member anyway, at 2 a.m. and took records from it. They also took crisps and sweets to keep the party swinging. At the time it was a big giggle.

Two hours later he was sober – and horrified.

Neither the boy nor any of his family had any record of

crime. This was an isolated, thoroughly stupid action, something to make one angry, not something deeply shocking. But in the eyes of the Law it was a crime. In the police mind there is no room for grace; the motto seems to be 'an eye for an eye, a tooth for a tooth'.

As I saw it, if this boy went to court he would be convicted and have, for always, a record. Moreover he would be tried as a criminal, which he wasn't – yet. This kind of situation can, and does, lead to a deep resentment not only against the police, but, far worse, against society as represented by the Law.

To the police he would be just someone who had broken the law and who should pay the full penalty. To those who knew him, he was an ordinary member of the community who, given the chance to make up for one idiotic piece of folly, could take a rightful place and play a useful part in it. This kind of conduct I put in the category of the old 'pinching the apples from the orchard' category, which was dealt with summarily on the spot. I realize the dangers of it, but if the old-fashioned policeman was able to use his powers of discretion in dealing with such cases, why shouldn't the present-day parson, who knows his flock better than the hard-pressed copper of 1967?

I took a chance. I said I would keep his secret and deal with the matter as best I could. I told him to bring me the records and what remained of the other stolen goods. I told him he must pay for what had been taken.

And so the Minister takes the loot back to the community centre at the earliest opportunity and asks to see the leader. But the C.I.D. are already there and interested to find the Minister arriving with stolen property. For the next ten days they try to find the culprit and are most displeased by my refusal to name him.

Who was right? Either of us?

A little while ago, there were four boys in the club who were heading for serious trouble. They were about fifteen years old and of low intelligence. Each came from a home which did not match up to any civilized definition of the word. They had a record of petty offences, such as stealing small quantities of copper from the electricity works and, after many hours of scraping it, selling it for a few shillings.

When they stole some lead they came up against the full pressure of the police, backed by local opinion in the street. The boys were habitually dishonest. They must be punished.

Society gets the criminals it deserves. When boys of this type come out of prison, they still have to come back into society. But on the whole they come back worse than when they went in. Their conduct was wrong and had to be punished, but the punishment would have been less necessary if the community had fulfilled its responsibilities towards such youngsters, the more because their homes had failed them. The youngsters themselves were irresponsible, but there they were, at fifteen, in the dock with all the might of the Law against them. Both in prison and when they came out they had to be someone's responsibility. In speaking on their behalf before the magistrate in court, I made this very point, and to my surprise and to the horror of the police, who had been after these particular boys for some time, they were not committed to Quarter Sessions but were allowed off with a small fine. Immediately and since, I have been looked upon with a certain amount of suspicion by the police. I can understand perfectly well why the policeman can only think in terms of black and white. He has no time to do otherwise, and sometimes the black by which he is faced is very black indeed, and for this reason he sees things a little out of proportion at times. However, my colleagues in the police force who know me reasonably well by this time would level the same charge against myself, I am sure.

Immediately after the court proceedings were finished in this particular case, I found myself with a real problem on my hands. Two of the boys, who came from a poor home in any case, were told by their father they were not going to be allowed to return. It has always intrigued me over the years how certain fathers, when faced with what they think are impossible children, have tried to solve the problem by making them somebody else's problem. In this case, the father in question made these boys my problem. I had talked in court about their being the community's responsibility, but I could not think of anybody in the community who would have been in a position to take these lads in. And so, as on several occasions previously, they had to be given lodgings on the church premises. Perhaps my motives were rather mixed in providing for their accommodation, because I knew the police were just waiting for the opportunity to say 'I told you so'. It would have been no use explaining to a gleeful copper, when one of these lads had done something criminal almost five minutes after being released from court, that I still believed I was right. Black is black and white is white, and ever will be so.

By its own failures, the community makes things more difficult for the policeman, who tends to become a purely punitive figure, someone who looks for trouble, someone who expects the worst and seems almost to hope for it. It is the wrong image. The policeman does not help matters when he deals brusquely, if not physically, as some do, with young people who hang about in the streets. If you don't know them, they look pretty wild and uncouth. Their manners are not of the best. The policeman, who does not know them and who is hard-pressed anyway, can only judge by appearances. When he pushes them on or plays them up, he is deepening their antagonism to authority, which is personified in his uniform. The old-time bobby in less complicated days might well have known Jimmy and Jill, known too that their father was a drunk and their mother a slut. This would not have justified any recalcitrance on the youngsters' part, but it would have helped the bobby to understand it and enabled him the better to deal with it.

Many policemen do try to take a pastoral interest in the youngsters they come across. This is greatly to their credit, because the system is all against them. They have to conform to regulations, orders and so on. As a result, many youngsters with deep resentments and feelings of rejection have had these increased by what seems the surliness of the hard-pressed copper, but which often enough is the expected reaction from any harassed person.

Nevertheless it is important not to be sentimental. Nobody who has come face to face with it can fail to realize what the police are up against with certain sick elements in our society. The youngster whose temper flares up and who resorts to his fists is one thing. Those who attack others, not excepting the police, with deliberate and extreme callousness and cruelty are quite another. We have known some of them in Lockleaze, and it is salutary to remember that the police are exposed to risk of such attacks, day in, day out.

It may well be true that, had he come to Britain, Hitler could have staffed his concentration camps from the local population. If it *is* true, society must surely consider how far such people are what they are by nature and how far they become so by reason of their environment – of their upbringing or lack of it. Some are so far gone by the age of eight or nine that even the most consummate pastoral approach by probation officers, police and the like would achieve little or nothing.

Whether we like it or not, no matter how respectable we are, we share a responsibility for the state of mind of these youngsters. Those who advocate the birch, the cat, even hanging, too often do so without any sense of their own guilt.

Which brings us back to the hypocrisy of society, a hypocrisy which is of no help in remedial work with the errant young. A boy may be fined £5 for stealing a bottle of milk. How much, one wonders, have the magistrates who impose the fine been able over the years to fiddle on their income tax? More than £5, perhaps? This may seem unfair pleading, but it is an idea which gets through to these youngsters, the idea that there is one rule for those who are on the right side of the law, another for those who are on the wrong side.

So often, in resentment – even desperation – the young hit first and then find that they have missed later because they aimed at the wrong target.

You and I cannot evade our share of the blame for both the hit and the miss. We are trying to evade the issue if in our club work we refuse them entry altogether.

The next chapter is the story of one 'hard case'. It is told simply to underline how demanding such characters can be and to provide an alibi for all those hard-pressed club leaders who simply have not the time to cope with such boys. They are a full-time job in themselves and our feeble attempts to involve ourselves with them have always been done at the expense of the rest of the club members.

9

Johnny Come Slowly

"BLOODY JUDGE," said Johnny, "five years for a bit of a barney. It's rough, bleeding rough!"

The victim of this 'injustice' had received his sentence for inflicting nine stab wounds on two of his enemies. To have tried to point out to Johnny that somebody might have been killed would have been a complete waste of time. He, who had injured someone the first time he had come into our youth club, would not have been impressed by such a sentiment. Johnny's first visit was to one of our weekly dance sessions. More than two hundred kids were enjoying themselves. It was past ten o'clock, and with less than an hour to go I was beginning to relax just a little.

But at a quarter past ten, such dreams were banished by the arrival of Johnny and his gang. There were a dozen of them, with their dead-pan faces, bizarre dress, and each with an earring in one ear. They were looking for trouble. It wasn't long coming. First there was the simulated insult, then the push, and then 'Who d'yer think yer shoving?' Then the battle commenced. Off came the belts, their studded belts, and in went the heads and boots.

The boys whose club it was, who felt at home in it, rallied round, and certainly gave as good as they got before the police arrived with commendable speed. Johnny's gang left by the emergency exit, leaving behind a trail of wreckage.

Several times in the last years I have seen at close quarters the way these characters fight. I have seen the butt to the head and the blood flow as the victim is pulled by the lapels of his jacket on to the forehead of his attacker. I have seen the knee arise with a dull thud into the groin and I have seen the 'victors' put the boot into the vanquished lying on the ground. This jungle law never fails to make me want to vomit. The immediate reaction, for once, seems right and I join momentarily the 'beat 'em, flog 'em, whip the skin off their backs' school of thought. The immediate and dangerous situation has to be met with force, simply to protect the weak, protect oneself, and to protect property. But the immediate need provides no long-term solution.

I wanted to discover a little more about what makes these boys tick, so, through certain useful contacts, a meeting was arranged with them on neutral territory. The place they chose was a tatty old pub in one of the slummiest parts of Bristol, now scheduled for demolition. It sported bare floors, rickety tables but no chairs. It was worse than a spit-and-sawdust saloon, there simply was no sawdust. In a room dignified by the name of Lounge they were gathered.

I was no more enamoured at seeing them 'socially' than I had been at our first encounter. As they drank pint after pint, as they pawed their women, as they tried all they knew to shock me – and partially succeeded, though I hope I did not show it – the terrible nausea was back again.

Johnny was there. He was the leader. His side-boards stretched three-quarters of the way down his cheek-bones. He wore dirty green jeans, and a mauve shirt open down to his waist, revealing a chest covered in the cheapest of tattoos.

This was his big moment. Not every day came the opportunity to 'take the mick' out of a parson in front of his mates.

"Good evening, vicar." He spat on the floor and we were off.

It would be dignifying it to call it a conversation. But I had not expected to converse. I wasn't that green. The most I hoped for was to establish some kind of relationship, and begin from there.

It is no good trying to reason with the likes of Johnny. To tell him his conduct had been thoroughly disgusting and reprehensible would have been a waste of breath. He and his boys had done it for kicks, and no other reason. A pretty perverted way of getting kicks, no doubt, but one that seems completely natural to them. And no amount of moralizing from me would have convinced them otherwise. Rotten parents, unstable childhood and environment, and a low I.Q. have all combined to make these kids what they are – and they cannot be argued out of what is to them a legitimate way of life.

One of the only hopes for them is to bring them somehow into collision with a new and superior environment, one strong enough to absorb them without crushing the life out of them. Obviously I am not referring to St Balderdash's down the road, or Holy Thingummybobs around the corner.

I stayed two hours simply looking for an opportunity to suggest a further meeting, and to try to maintain the contact now established.

It came near the end of the evening. Johnny told me that he had already arranged for a large gang to come up in three furniture vans the following week to continue the good work. I said my boys wouldn't like that "Like f . . . they wouldn't," agreed Johnny.

Desperately, I said any fool could collect a mob together and fight about nothing at all. A wise man took counsel first to discover if there were issues worth fighting over.

It was the first parsonic, pious remark I had unleashed all night – which surely isn't bad for a chap ordained several years ago – but to my amazement it worked.

Johnny was quite prepared to have a council of war. The idea appealed to him enormously. And so, finally, it was agreed that three of my boys would meet himself and two of his boys. But where?

I suggested they should meet at my manse behind the church.

They were worried. How could I guarantee them a free passage into my 'territory'? I offered to drive them up in my car, and after it was all over to take them out of my 'territory' in the same way.

How could I guarantee they wouldn't be 'done over' by my boys, having got to my place?

My word was their only guarantee. They were not too happy about that, but they agreed to come. They warned me that if they came to any harm, negotiations would cease forthwith.

I was learning fast, and told them the day my boys did not do as I told them would be the day I resigned and turned my collar back to a more normal position. They seemed to understand this, and the time and the place were fixed.

The following Wednesday I duly picked them up in the car. They had already managed to drink several pints apiece. I began to wonder what excuse could be offered if we were stopped by the police.

They kept very quiet on the way out. We drove down the side of the church to my garage. I got out first. They followed slowly, suspiciously. I had arranged for my three boys to call fifteen minutes later, and fortunately there was no one in sight.

"Seems to be O.K.", murmured Johnny. "Let's go in."

In we went. They looked around my study cautiously for a minute or two. "You do a lot of reading?" said Johnny, gazing suspiciously at the bookshelves. "A little," I replied.

He looked at a Picasso print on the wall. He shook his head sadly. "You're not a very good painter, are you?" I had to admit I was not very good. I was not very amused then, because I had seen what they were carrying. Johnny must have caught my glance, for he said, "O.K., boys, his reverence was right. We got here safe. Hand them over."

They hesitated. Then they agreed, and out came three of the ugliest-looking knives I ever wish to see.

"Thank you very much," I said, trying to sound as if the best man had just handed me the ring. I put them in a drawer. There was a pause. They smoked.

"Done any time, Johnny?" I tried to sound casual.

"Two years."

"Why?"

"Knocking down a copper."

"What with?"

"A car."

"An accident?"

He laughed. " 'Course not, I went for him in it."

"I see."

We all meditated on this one for a minute and then the bell went. I let my side in. They were no angels, but at least they never carried weapons. We must be thankful for small mercies, I suppose.

Both groups of three sat facing each other.

At least to begin with I had the advantage. Their dislike for each other was temporarily forgotten while they adjusted themselves to the unusual environment. I seized the initiative while the mood lasted. I explained briskly why they were there. There had been a dance. Into this dance the gang had walked. Representatives of the gang were with us tonight. There had been a fight, which had been broken up. There was a possibility of more trouble. This was an unhappy state of affairs. I, for one, could not see the point. Would not the sensible thing be to talk about our differences?

I knew it was already beginning to sound like a Bible Class. Johnny's face was split into a callous sneer. He had forgotten his feeling of strangeness, for he spat into the fire and said, "We're bringing three van-loads of the boys up on Friday." We pondered this for a few moments as the fire sizzled away.

"You bring three van-loads up", snarled Eddie, "and we'll castrate the f...ing lot of you." This was a counterblast to my Bible Class approach all right, but it was no more of a help in solving the problems.

At 8 p.m., when conversation had lasted ten minutes, I had already given up hope. But this simply showed how green I was. For by 10 o'clock the mood was more optimistic. They had gone over the same ground a hundred times. They had uttered threat and counter-threat. I had been ignored completely for thirty minutes at one stretch as they shouted and yelled, never quite coming to blows, however. I had made three lots of coffee. They had gone through one hundred and twenty of my cigarettes (I had not smoked for a twelvemonth, but I had fifteen myself that night). After two hours, neither side thought they had conceded one bit to the enemy, but what they did not see was that a relationship was beginning to be struck up. Johnny still threatened the three van-loads, Eddie still threatened to castrate the lot. But Johnny began to agree it might not be a bad thing if Eddie castrated old Butch for a start. Crude jokes were cracked. I was prepared to laugh at anything provided they kept on laughing too. And to my utter amazement, I began to discover that bonds were being formed between the two sides. By 11 p.m. the miracle was there for all to see, and it simply needed a stack of canned beer to seal the friendships formed.

Now completely relaxed, Johnny tried to rationalize their behaviour.

"It's like this, see. We've all been 'inside'. There are no clubs for us. They don't want us. When we arrive at the door they tell us to clear off. If only you'd let us into your dances, we'd be O.K., you'll see."

I explained that we were not a closed club, but they were boys from a different district. They could not expect to wander into our club and not be looked on with suspicion by our boys. They knew as well as we did that a district was a district, and groups of more than six itinerant strangers were just asking for trouble if they wandered uninvited into other clubs.

We agreed that certainly in their districts there was nothing for them. But they also said all their mob, the ones I had seen in the pub, had all recently done time. This they had in common, and they intended to do jobs together in the future. They were all unemployed, but they didn't want to work. Why should they work? By this time I thought I knew them sufficiently well to say I did not think it surprising that certain clubs did not allow them inside the premises. They were quite a fearsome-looking bunch, and though they had mellowed a little in the manse, I still had no illusions about them.

The immediate problem was solved, but I found myself with a bigger one on my plate. These kids were just heading for Borstal again, and eventually prison. There was nothing to stop them being old lags before they were thirty. But I also realized that each one of them was a full-time job in himself. It

103

is not the parson's job to combine in his own person the role of probation officer, after-care worker, social worker and all the rest, but even when he is co-operating with the said people and trying to help the boys like Johnny, even such combined efforts are often stretched to the full. I remember reading an article in *New Society* a few months ago in which an experiment in New York was described. In this experiment, a group of social workers decided to concentrate on a group of delinquent boys who had all been in trouble with the police. The aim was to allocate one social worker to one boy and each worker would be concerned for his lad every day of every week for six months. At the end of six months, they compared notes, and compared their group of boys who had had this specialized treatment with a similar group of boys who had had the normal contact, which, of necessity was the usual casual one from the hard-pressed social worker. Even within six months, the results were extraordinary. Those boys who had had full attention showed some response to the care that had been lavished upon them, whereas the other group were no better off. As any probation officer will tell you, the Johnnies of this world are a full-time job in themselves, and I certainly know this from experience, as Johnny, for the next two years, led me a merry dance. I decided to concentrate on Johnny, because even then I was not naïve enough to think I could cope with the whole group, and I certainly realized the congregation was not ready to cope with the whole group and face up to all the other problems as well.

I wish I could say the story of Johnny had a happy ending, but the ending, or the beginning, is not yet in sight. For the record, however, I would mention that all other nine members of the gang have ended up in prison since our meeting, but not Johnny. It has been a close thing with him. He has been on one charge since, not too serious a one compared with some of his past misdemeanours, but at the same time with his record one for which he could have been heavily punished. But thanks to a sympathetic judge, who saw that something was happening, he was not sent down. I can still see Johnny standing in the dock waiting for the judge to make up his mind and to hear just how long it would be this time.

The judge looked up. "I have considered all that has been said on your behalf and I am going to give you a conditional discharge."

Johnny did not move a muscle and stood rooted to the spot, staring fixedly into space.

The judge again looked up. 'Well, what are you waiting for?"

"I'm waiting for my sentence, my Lord."

The judge smiled. "Haven't you heard of conditional discharge? Don't you know what it is?"

"No, sir."

"Well, you are free to go away and find out!"

10

'When Does the Programme Begin?'

AFTER THE passion play had been widely performed, many people beat a path to our door to see this great club which had come to pass. On some occasions they struck lucky and came on a night when everything, to use the parlance of those days, was swinging. But there were many more who, entering our doors and expecting to find it all laid on a plate for them in the course of one hour, were confronted by the spectacle of a handful of youngsters playing table-tennis and a few girls dancing in desultory fashion. They have gone away with the air of 'Who do they think they're kidding?', though we have never attempted to kid anyone.

Even when our casual visitors have found the premises crammed almost to the roof, they are still not necessarily impressed. One Sunday evening a lady who had attended the service came into the club afterwards. Having been offered a seat and a cup of tea by one of the club members, she sat and watched the dancing, the games-playing and the social groupings that were going on all around her. It was one of those evenings which my colleagues and I enjoy, which go well from start to finish. It was also the sort of evening which can never be guaranteed to repeat itself, even with exactly the same company, on the following night. We make the most of them when they occur. And this particular one was as relaxed and carefree a time as we could have wished. But after half an hour the lady in question, looking puzzled, said "When does the programme begin?" I explained that there was no programme and that we never ever had a programme. She soon took her departure.

The fact that we never have a programme does not imply that we disapprove of such an approach. By a programmed evening I mean one in which most of the time is given over to organized activities of one nature or another, anything from needlework to weight-lifting. But most church clubs, including our own, have not the premises, never mind the trained staff and the necessary finance, to engage in such pursuits. If we had more resources, we could and should engage in more programmed activities. To do so at the present stage would result only in the severance of existing relationships with a whole host of boys and girls.

The Duke of Edinburgh Award scheme can illustrate the pitfalls which await the club leader who attempts to provide the facilities necessary for such an undertaking. Many such leaders have discovered to their cost that the Edinburgh Award involves a great deal of time and paperwork, some would say too much, in proportion to the results it makes possible. The leader often has to concentrate on one candidate, maybe the one white sheep, while the other ninety-nine are tearing the place to bits for lack of anyone around to take an interest in them. Such schemes may be all very well for the highly organized club with adequate financial resources behind it, but even there they can be an irritant and stand between the leaders and the majority of their members.

It is also imperative that the existing local situation should be taken into account whenever any church or voluntary body is thinking about 'doing youth work'. Too much unnecessary time and money is spent on duplicating facilities in districts where the pooling of all resources would be the more effective and right thing to do. In our own area there is already in existence a club which meets on several evenings in the local comprehensive school. Until we came to our senses, we were duplicating our programmes and attempting to provide two clubs in close proximity to each other, each offering activities plus a social evening. The result was a growing rivalry in the race for membership and a wrong kind of competitive spirit.

All this was arrested with the co-operation of a progressive headmaster and through the influence of the Newsom Report.[1] The result has been that we began to look at the parish youth work as a whole. Nowadays the school concentrates on the activities for which it has ample premises and staffing, as well as some basic social amenities to go with such activities. We concentrate more on the social side, providing a meeting place for youngsters in the large hall, and in an adjoining and reasonably spacious coffee bar. We also run four football teams in amateur league football.

So when the casual visitor looks in on our premises he has certainly not seen the whole picture. He is, for instance, not aware that some of those who are lounging around are members of the football teams; as such they are attending the school gymnasium for training on Wednesday nights under a professional instructor. Nor is he aware that several of the others are members of sheet-metal classes, cookery classes, art appreciation classes, craft classes and several more, all available at the school at the top of the road. Of course there are many others present who engage in no activities whatsoever, but they have to be looked after as well. Amongst this group are certainly the street-corner type of boy or girl, many a youngster from an unstable home background, possessed of not very much initiative and with little interest in anything constructive.

But too many people are quick off the mark in condemning all the youngsters in this grouping. By no means all of them are layabouts and even the layabouts have to be loved and indeed are often the most lovable. Some of the others in this grouping work quite hard as apprentices, labourers or technicians. They have a healthy disregard for the attitude of mind which holds that they should always be doing something. Imagine what the reaction would be from many an adult, or college boy for that matter, if he belonged to a club or social group whose committee was always insisting that he should engage in an activity. Many of our youngsters are fully involved with their careers, their love-life and so on. They appreciate

Half our Future, H.M. Stationery Office, 1963.

an atmosphere in which they can relax and not be pushed around by the born organizer.

The policy of 'keeping them off the streets' is often condemned as a negative approach to youth work, but we should not be too quick to condemn it out of hand. I only wish that more churches would even start with this in mind when they are thinking of engaging in youth work. Once they did, they would very soon find that they were involved in work of a more positive nature.

It all depends of course in what kind of area such churches find themselves. There is all the difference in opportunity between, for instance, the present-day city of Bristol and Luton, Bedfordshire. Whereas the former provides a host of facilities to absorb the attention and the money of the young, places such as the latter have nothing like the same attractions. When I drive through some of our sleepy market towns and expanding villages, I often think what an opportunity there is for the local churches if they were willing to open their halls without too many preconceived ideas as to what they were trying to do. Where there exist no rival commercial attractions, there are also boundless opportunities, as we found at Lockleaze in the early days. It really is a question of playing a situation by ear and being adaptable. For instance, now that the centre of Bristol is a real meeting place for young people, we as a church club occasionally invade their sanctuary by taking over a central dance hall and running the dance under the name and aegis of the church.

I would go so far as to say however that in places like Luton, and a whole string of such come to mind, if one or two church halls are not being used on two nights a week to cater for young people, then the church does not deserve that they should come within earshot. We are far too anxious to cater for young people simply on our terms, and they will have none of it. We are not prepared, as often as we should be, to put up with the inconvenience and the risks which are undoubtedly involved when we open our premises for their use. Many a reader could perhaps recite from painful experience the petty,

109

narrow-minded reasons given by church authorities and church members as to why the young people should not have the run of the premises. These vary from 'They don't respect the property' to 'You'd think they owned the place'. So it is that we quiet our consciences and make straight the path for religion.

In some areas there will be no need to keep youngsters off the streets because this task has been done for us, and not as badly as some people would like to think. But there are still many where young people have no real meeting places except the streets or the pubs. These provide a tremendous opportunity, if the church is willing to take it.

Our own work at Lockleaze, which has often started from the point of simply providing a meeting place for young people, we tend to describe, as far as adult participation is concerned, as that of propping up a wall for the Kingdom's sake and on occasion having to leap off the very same wall for the very same Kingdom's sake. The adults are present but are not there to intrude too much or impose themselves upon the young. They are there to show a face, to answer questions when they are asked and to ensure that the centre is a warm meeting place and not just a bear-garden. From this seemingly casual approach worthwhile relationships have emerged. Young people need strong moments in their lives – what I believe the psychologists call concretism. This partially explains the wild way some of them search for kicks. But there can really be no substitute for a wholesome relationship with an adult who does not seek to impose himself upon them but who all the same eventually wins for himself an authority which the youngster is willing to accord him. This is why I have no sympathy at all with that view of youth work which implies that the adult should be not only in the background but almost non-existent.

In youth leadership circles there has been much discussion on this particular topic, and words such as 'permissive' and 'self-determination' and 'control' are bandied about. A controlled club is one in which the rules are rigidly drawn up.

Within them the life of the club must operate. These rules cover such matters as the maximum number of members the club should have before a waiting list is started, what is the age limit, what is the procedure for engaging in activities or pursuits of one kind or another, what are the penalties for non-payment of subscriptions, and so on. The advantage of this kind of club is that everybody knows where he stands, provided of course young people are willing to find out where they stand according to rules drawn up by people other than themselves.

Then there is the philosophy of 'self-determination', which seems to be a view held by several young men straight out of training college and therefore has to be examined seriously as possibly the official line of youth work. I suspect that these young men have not got hold of the right end of the stick from their college training. In practice what they mean by it is as follows: the youth club is the young people's club and they therefore have a right to determine by themselves, without benefit of adult help, how it should be run and what they should do. Of course they will make mistakes, but they must learn by their mistakes and basic policies should come from them and be implemented by their own actions. They shall decide what time the club opens, what time it closes, what the subscription shall be, and it shall all be done democratically by majority vote, though the general policy of the club shall be in the hands of a young people's committee elected by the annual general meeting.

Now this philosophy has a lot to commend it and I go along with it to a certain point. Where I sharply disagree is on its emphasis, at least in the mouths of certain youth leaders, on the need for the adult voice and face to be almost totally in the background. My own view is that permissive behaviour is the best philosophy in almost every situation. By this I mean that so much is permitted under the rules or the no-rule of self-determination, but that there are definite boundaries and demarcation lines which cannot be drawn by the young people themselves and which have to be drawn by them in co-opera-

111

tion with the adults. The self-determinationists hold up their hands in horror at this, crying that this is imposed authority from above.

I am not against imposed authority so long as it is a benevolent authority. Sometimes we owe such to our young charges. But I would say that under wise leadership a corporate authority emerges which exercises its own restraints and agreed penalties. The mutual respect and co-operation of young and old is necessary if this stage is to be reached, usually after many years of endeavour. Such a state often does away with the need for a permanent committee which decides policy. In a genuinely family club it is generally known what the real requirements are without benefit of resolutions and amendments.

I can best describe what I call permissive behaviour by giving as an illustration our junior club. This is the breeding-ground for our senior clubs, and for much more if we care to let it take place. The ages range from those who are just turned eleven to those who are nearing their fourteenth birthday. At that age, and unless you have two adults to every child, you just cannot begin to arrest their attention and to occupy them in quiet pursuits. We can muster a staff of, on average, ten every Wednesday night. At the height of the winter we have about a hundred juniors in the large hall, which for two hours resembles a bumper fun palace and indoor playground, or as some have described it, a jungle. The record-player blares away, young girls dance with each other, boys play table-tennis and billiards after a fashion. In the midst of all this, scores of youngsters rush around, scream, fight, jump off chairs and on to chairs, besiege the refreshment counter and throughout keep up a deafening din.

When the casual visitor has entered our premises on a Wednesday evening, he has often quailed visibly. One expressed deep disgust that we could not occupy children in more worthwhile pursuits than those which he saw on that particular evening. And yet we do not go far enough to satisfy our logical self-determination friends, because there are limits which the youngsters know exist and which they respect, except on those few occasions when they are very naughty. They know they are not allowed to tear the blinds or harm the property deliberately or to attack others with malicious intent. In all the years this club has been functioning I can only remember a few instances of deliberate damage, although our casual visitors have gone away with the impression that the juniors were systematically tearing down the church brick by brick. Interestingly enough, many of the friendships which have grown between the adults and the young people have begun amidst such a bear-garden, and a mutual trust has been established which has blossomed forth into real friendship and respect in later years. Young people want to know where they stand and what the boundaries are, and they have a right to be told all this. We owe it to them as persons. This is not to say they are not to be allowed to make what we think are mistakes, but it is to say it *is* their right to expect our help when they've made them, and even when in danger of making them.

Recently I was engaged in counselling a teenager who was in a great deal of trouble at home, who had been involved with the police on several occasions and was now on probation. He came to see me at a set time once a week and spent the time pouring out his tale of woe against all those people who, as he thought, did not understand him. One evening, he decided to come up on spec instead of on his usual night, and as he arrived at the front door I was on my way out to accompany one of our football teams to an evening match. For the occasion I was sensibly dressed in collar and tie and had discarded my clerical collar. Usually I am seen more often in my clerical collar than in a collar and tie in the parish. I noticed with surprise the look on the boy's face as he saw me in this unfamiliar dress, but as I was in a hurry, I simply said "I'm sorry, I haven't time to speak to you now, but you are coming tomorrow night in any case. Will it wait until then?" As I rushed by, he said "I suppose so."

The next night he came to the house in a rage. I asked him

what was the matter, suspecting that it was my brusque farewell of the previous evening which had upset him. But that was not the case. He said to me in a voice trembling with emotion "Don't you not never wear that collar again." "What collar?" I said. "That tie thing," he said. Now, ignoring the implication of a treble negative, he was demanding that I should never appear in a collar and tie again, but that I should appear in my true colours as a parson. He had come to me as a parson for help and it was in that capacity that he felt safe with me. When he saw that after all I was only an ordinary man, this shook his confidence. To him the collar symbolized an authority which he craved, and he thought that I had been deceiving him. Bruce Kenrick tells the following story in his book *Come out the Wilderness*.[2]

On a rainy Saturday evening one of the pastors turned into 104th Street and stopped short in surprise at the sight of a member of his church; the man was very drunk.

"Hi, Flacco," said the minister to the gaunt, wild-eyed figure who stood blocking his path.

Flacco gazed back sullenly, and then, for some strange, twisted reason, burst out with the sudden protest:

"Listen, you dirty priest. This Jesus guy. He's a swine!" He swayed nearer the pastor and then cried out again, "Jesus is a swine! Jesus is a swine!" Flacco was shouting at the top of his voice and his words were like slashes from a razor's edge, leaving the pastor wounded and weak and utterly confused. How to defend his Lord against this man? How to defend God's Son? Then suddenly he felt convinced that his job was not to defend. His role was to accept; to accept old Flacco precisely as he was, without hint of condemnation. "Jesus is a swine!" The pastor's whole attitude changed. He relaxed. He stood there in a drizzle of rain, feeling as though the cries were biting deeply into his flesh, but believing, as Flacco finally shambled off, that God's will had been done.

But had it? It turned out that at all events Flacco's will had not been done. The pastor called on him next day.

"Come in. Reverend," he said gravely, motioning him to sit down on an unmade bed beside the stove. They both sat in silence

[2] Fontana Books, p. 105.

114

for what seemed like five minutes, before Flacco looked up and asked, "Why didn't you knock me down last night?" He really meant what he said. He meant it, perhaps, because he wanted boundaries to be set round his undisciplined life, and he wanted the security of knowing they were boundaries which must not be crossed. Flacco had publicly confessed his faith in Christ, and if he abused his Lord, he hoped that his pastor would knock him down.

I just cannot accept the self-determinationists' line that the youngsters themselves decide on what the boundaries are. On the other hand, I certainly decry the kind of imposed authority which many youth leaders and church authorities consider to be legitimate when they are discussing their approach to youth work. In fact, where youngsters are concerned, you just cannot impose an authority from above and hope that they will respond in the way you want. The authority of which I am thinking is an authority which is given to a person because he has earned it. A great deal of church youth policy is still laid down by parochial church councils, deacons and elders or management committees who have hardly any contact with the actual club members. Young people, even the hardest of cases, can and will respond to the person who really cares for them and who is prepared to put up with a great deal from them in his attempt to stand alongside them and be their friend. Indeed it is a two-way relationship; they learn from him and he learns from them, but to think that youngsters can do without an adult voice and determine their own policy is to give them less than their due.

Of course, we must remember that there is a difference between being involved with a person and being identified with a person. We adults are not called upon and should not be expected to be identified with young people. I mean by this trying to be as they are, to share their interests completely and perhaps even to dress in the style in which they dress. If we try to identify ourselves in this way, the youngster is the first to see through us. He wants us to be ourselves and he demands this of us. We owe him this much. Anyway, whenever we do

115

attempt to identify ourselves with them, we can never go far enough, and the result is just ridiculous in the youngster's, as well as in our adult colleagues', eyes.

I remember when winkle-picker shoes, the sharp-pointed variety, were very fashionable, I thought it would be a good idea if I bought a pair. But I was sufficiently aware that to buy the authentic article, although it might have identified me with the young people, would have certainly disidentified me with my own adult grouping and especially from my clerical colleagues. So I tried to strike the happy medium but all the same bought a pair of shoes which I considered to be very daring.

I was wearing them for the first time in the club and speaking to Harry. I crossed my legs and waggled my foot around waiting for his comments. As none were forthcoming, I drew his attention to the shoes. "What do you think of them?" "They're all right, I suppose," he said, "if you like that sort of thing." "What do you mean?" I said, "if you like that sort of thing. Don't you think they're pretty sharp?" He looked at them for a second, then said, "Gaan, they're still in the box you bought them in."

It is wrong to try and identify ourselves with young people; they want us to be ourself, though not a self divorced from them altogether. This is what involvement means. It means being prepared to be ourselves, proud to be ourselves, but to stand where others are without accepting in every detail the culture of the others, or even approving of it in every detail. It also means standing alongside others in love, but at the same time being prepared to judge them.

In that same chapter of Bruce Kenrick's from which I have just quoted, there is another incident which underlines this theme. Luis Cortez, a young Puerto Rican, was working as a full-time leader with one of the Harlem street churches.

When his group of teenagers burst into the church hall one evening, Luis took one look at the crate of stolen apples which they carried so triumphantly and his response did not look like 'acceptance'. "So!" he blazed out furiously. "You meet here in the church and you go out and raid the stores. You think you're smart. I tell you, you're fools! One day you'll do this and the cops'll come. And when they come they'll shoot. They won't care whether they plug you in the leg or in the heart." The group stood motionless as Luis glared round at them. "And listen. I'll tell you something. You can't believe in God and then go and steal someone's apples. It's *wrong*. You just can't do it!" His voice was rising with anger. "You know what you are? You're all *thieves*! That's what you are. Every one of you's a thief!" and he pointed at them one by one, his accusing finger jabbing the air just short of every startled face. "You're a *thief*! *Thief! Thief! Thief! Thief!* . . ."

This was authority and ministry and grace, and, undoubtedly, judgment. But it was a judgment which did not reject the boys who continued to meet with Luis in the church. In other words, Luis still accepted those who were thieves although his judgment of them was absolute.[3]

And so the kind of policy which we pursue at St James', Lockleaze, and the one with which we are most in agreement, is one of permissive leadership. The young people are allowed to do what they like within certain limits, but the limits are clearly defined. When David said in chapter four, " 'e lets us do what we wanna do, you know, beyond reason", he meant 'within reason'. He knew what the limits were even though they had never been written down in rules and regulations.

One last word on the policy of self-determination. It is interesting to notice that when the adult face has been absent from certain events, then those events, if not (as some have) ending in chaos, have in many instances bordered on the chaotic. The sole league football match in which one of our teams participated and which had to be abandoned before the end, even in the presence of a professional referee, was the only occasion when no adult had been present on the touch line. The situation would never have built up to the stage which it reached if there had been present at least one adult known to the boys. The following letter was sent to us, following a complaint by the referee to the league authority concerning one

[3] Ibid., pp. 104–5.

117

of the culprits, a member of our team, who was sent off before the final *débâcle*. It never ceases to cause amusement to my colleagues and myself.

Dear Sir,

I have to advise you that I am in receipt of a referee's report stating that Jeff Ingleby (St James') was ordered from the field of play for a dangerous tackle on an opponent after previously being warned. After some argument he left the field of play but returned within a minute, advising the referee that he would have to put him off the pitch. The referee then abandoned the game.

Any statement by the player or club should reach me within the next seven days. This case will come before the Council at the next meeting.

Yours faithfully,

Hon. Gen. Secretary

The phrase 'advising the referee that he would have to put him off the pitch' is surely a classic euphemism. You need not read between the lines to know that with a great deal of difficulty and arguing and swearing and fighting was that lad sent off the pitch, whereupon he immediately returned to cause a further disturbance. Your self-determinationist would say that it is only through this kind of thing that the lad will learn and the rest of the team will learn. This is nonsense. They learn nothing except how to cause chaos, engage in a jolly good punch-up, and ruin an afternoon.

11

Postscript

By Mark Hankey

MY JOB is very different from Ernest Marvin's. My people (to use the name he has for his lively flock at Lockleaze) are subject to and within reason submit to a disciplinary code of which their fee-paying parents approve; indeed it is part of their motive for sending their sons to my school. My lot are young and all of one sex. They come, in the main, from what are called 'good homes'. Ernest's young are older, both in years and in experience for their years. Unless they have been to Borstal, they have no knowledge of that discipline which obtains in a school designed mainly for boarders. Their parents could probably not have afforded the fees – nor thought them worth paying. Their homes vary widely in quality, from the very good to the rather bad.

In some ways I envy Ernest. When I fail, as too often, it seems it really must be my own fault. When he succeeds, it is a triumph.

His most publicized success has been *A Man Dies*. The first time we saw this astonishing presentation, my wife and I sat silent at the end. If others had not broken the spell by moving, I believe we could have remained so for some time. The challenge implicit in the play had hit us pretty hard.

For a few years I had been experimenting with light music for religious purposes. It had not occurred to me that rock and roll could be used for the same purposes to such exciting effect. I did not suppose that my own music, which has its roots in

Rodgers and Gershwin, rather than Lennon and McCartney, would have any appeal to the jiving cast of *A Man Dies*. But it did seem that I might be barking up the lower branches of Marvin's tree and, on the advice of one or two friends who knew him, I invited him to come to my house.

It may be partly because our communities are so different that we have found each other good company. It is refreshing for each to visit the other's manor. Ernest has preached a series of brilliant sermons to my school. My kids have enjoyed them and always look forward to the next one. I have been to Lockleaze on a variety of occasions, sometimes as a casual member of the congregation of St James' – always made kindly welcome by the elders, always stimulated by the vitality of the worship. There is never a dull moment in these services; they are taken at break-neck speed and with a most inspiring sincerity. The younger members of the congregation may, for the most part, resemble the audience in a down-town cinema and behave as such. But God is there all right and you can talk with him.

There have been times when I have been able to contribute to these uncommon occasions. Once I was asked to preach. The next day I lost my voice and did not regain it for some three months. I have often wondered whether this was Divine Judgment in action.

On another occasion I took Sol Raye to Lockleaze. Sol is a West Indian singer whose voice uncannily resembles that of the late Nat 'King' Cole and who had sung my settings of Magnificat and Nunc Dimittis in, amongst other churches, Salisbury Cathedral. He sang them at Lockleaze, and also the Lord's Prayer from the Mancroft Mass.

Then there was the day on which I held a congregational practice before the service and taught them the Baptism song from 'Songs for Bermuda', so that we could all sing 'Hey, Little Baby' to the five infants who were baptized during the service.

Perhaps the most exciting evening was that on which I took to St James' Paul Danquah, whom many of the congregation had seen playing opposite Rita Tushingham in the film *A Taste of Honey*. Ernest had asked Paul to read a passage from one of the Epistles, which Paul did with dignity and sensitivity. There was an unusual and most moving hush as he read. He was conscious of this, I know, for when he had finished, he stood quite still as if unconscious of his surroundings. It was a pleasantly ecumenical occasion too. Paul is a Roman Catholic, I am an Anglican, and the preacher was the Moderator of the General Assembly of the Presbyterian Church of England.

Paul and Sol Raye stayed on after the services to entertain in the club, Sol to sing and Paul to recite negro poetry. I have quite often been to this Sunday club myself and have sung my own songs at the piano. I have also talked, played and argued at meetings of younger groups on other evenings in the week. There is a sense in which I should be quite well-known up at Lockleaze.

Nevertheless, though I am always given a friendly welcome by older members both in church and club, I have failed to make friends with any of the younger element except for Valerie Mountain, whom I admire both as a singer and as a person, and Ron Baker, who is a musician and can take over the organ when my low music is being sung. This failure is partly, I believe, because the turn-over of young people is so rapid: there are lots of young faces every time I go there, but I do not recognize them any more than they seem to know mine. I like the young and want to talk with them, but I do not communicate successfully at Lockleaze. I'm all wrong, of course. Not just my age. My clothes are wrong (they would be whatever I wore), my accent is wrong (I often wonder whether Ernest realizes how useful to him is his Scots intonation), my language is wrong (if I chose to draw on them, even my expletives would be), my dancing is not only wrong but funny (I always want to dance when a good group is playing), my whole approach is wrong. I'm like a copper in a coffee-bar, a beak in an approved school. I'm a square in their circle.

Ernest, of course, can communicate like wildfire in my set-up. That is partly because he is a much better communicator than I am, partly because my lot put on their angel-masks

121

when visitors come and, in most cases, enjoy responding. By and large I have found that I can communicate with people of all types, and I wonder whether my almost complete failure to do so at Lockleaze is any measure of the difficulty of Ernest's task. Of all barriers, that of suspicion is hardest to break down, of all clouds those of doubt and uncertainty are the most difficult to dispel. Those kids, all dancing in their unique and often technically brilliant style, seem happy enough. But in fact even their own happiness may be teetering on a cliff's edge. At any moment the knives may be out.

The chips on the shoulders of the all-too-distinct sections of our society are a horrible impediment. There are too many sections anyway, and none will admit to its own chip. I suppose that when I go to Lockleaze and try to mix with young men whose hair is as long as their trousers are tight and with girls whose hair is shorter than their mini-skirts, their chip tells them that I'm the patronizing outsider, the interfering do-gooder, the phoney oldster who thinks he can shoot a line with the young – who are real. My chip tells me that I must not be natural, that I must try to say the sort of things they say (which, of course, I can't) and that I must endeavour to break down social barriers by pretending they don't exist (which, alas, they do).

When I get away, my chip weighs less heavily and stops putting such ideas into my head. Then I believe that I could, if I was there more often, achieve some small break-through. I'm an optimist. Perhaps I should stay in my own community, which I know and where I am within reason accepted.

But that's the trouble. We all do that.

A couple of years ago I was concerned in the musical side of a mission to the parish of St Andrew's, Hartcliffe, another of Bristol's housing estates. One afternoon the vicar, Derek Palmer, and Father Gerard Beaumont, C.R., who was also taking part in the mission, came to my house for a cup of tea. They said they wanted me to write a pop song about death. At first I took this as a joke and said that if they would give me a few minutes I would run it up for them. But they were serious.

That evening Ernest Marvin came to see me and I put my problem to him. Quite soon we produced a title – 'Dying to live' – then, after we had had a fortnight or so in which to mull the idea in our brains, we happened to travel together in a train from Bristol to London. During the journey, stimulated by British Railways' coffee and, I hope, by a more potent inspiration, we produced a complete lyric for the song. That afternoon I showed the words to Toni Ross, a talented, if disorganized, pop musician, and he composed the tune.

'Dying to live' is the only pop song I know that has a text. 'We know that we have passed from death unto life, because we love our brethren' (I John 3.14). It is really a sermon in the pop idiom.

The theme of it, which is that a man must die again and again if he is fully to live, seems to me relevant to the problems which Ernest Marvin faces at Lockleaze. Society, which includes the young people of Ernest's parish, may pay lip-service to the historical fact that A Man Died, but it will not accept the much more important and relevant one that A Man Dies – now, to-day. And those few who do accept this second fact are willing to let him die for them without bothering to draw one of the vital conclusions of this – Resurrection. For the resurrection reveals the point of Christ's death. He died to live again. We too must die if we are to live as he lives.

The little deaths which society must die in order to live, the little sacrifices which it must make in order to achieve its proper purpose, seem still beyond its powers of responsibility. It is easy to blame the Haves for not giving and the Have-nots for being bloody-minded about not getting. The plain fact remains that society is selfish and self-seeking. It has still to learn to love.

> Say, can you love when you're hurt, brother?
> Or when you're rubbed in the dirt, brother?
> If not, it's got to be said
> You're dead.

We can't. And so we are.

This, to Mr Square looking into Mr Circle of Lockleaze, seems to be the core of the bitter-sweet apple at which Ernest Marvin and Brian Phillips and their friends are so faithfully and courageously biting. It is a big apple and hard to bite, but they have taken sizeable chunks out of it.